INTELLECTUAL FERMENT
FOR POLITICAL REFORMS
IN TAIWAN, 1971-1973

Mab Huang

密西根中國研究集刊

MICHIGAN PAPERS IN CHINESE STUDIES
28   1976

THE UNIVERSITY OF MICHIGAN
CENTER FOR CHINESE STUDIES

MICHIGAN PAPERS IN CHINESE STUDIES
NO. 28

by

Center for Chinese Studies
The University of Michigan

Printed in the United States of America

INTELLECTUAL FERMENT FOR POLITICAL
REFORMS IN TAIWAN, 1971-1973

by
Mab Huang

Ann Arbor

Center for Chinese Studies
The University of Michigan

1976

CONTENTS

PREFACE

The early seventies marked a turning point in the fortune of the ruling party and the government of the Republic of China in Taiwan. After two decades of firm control and security, the gov-

first time in twenty years took it upon themselves to agitate for basic political reforms. They called for an open and democratic society and demanded wide-ranging changes. They organized demonstrations, held forums, signed petitions, and made speeches. It was an exciting time. For a while it appeared that they might achieve what they had set out to do. This, however, did not come to pass. The ruling party and government responded with partial accommodations and selective reprisals. For all practical purposes, the ferment for political reforms had subsided by the summer of 1973.

This study is an attempt to reconstruct the intellectual ferment for political reforms in the years 1971-1973. In particular, it focuses on the description and analysis of the aspirations, hopes, and fears of the young university professors and students, the programs they proposed, the actions they took, their relations with the ruling party and government, and their impact and achievements. It is hoped that such an account will not only shed light on the politics of Taiwan, a subject generally neglected by Western scholars, but also contribute to our knowledge of intellectuals in times of crisis under an authoritarian political system.

This study began to develop in the academic year 1971-1972 while I was on sabbatical leave and teaching at my alma mater, National Taiwan University. During my sojourn there, the ferment for political reforms was reaching its height. It was my good fortune that many university professors and students playing a crucial role in the agitation were either good friends or my students. I had the opportunity of participating in their meetings, observing them closly in action, and interviewing them at length. To a moderate degree, I also supported them in their effort, as described in these pages.

Upon my return to the United States in August 1972, I started work on this manuscript. I was primarily motivated by the desire to clarify for myself what the intellectual ferment for political reforms was about; to a lesser degree, I desired to attest, as objectively as possible, to the efforts of the young intellectuals in Taiwan. I reviewed the literature on politics in Taiwan and carefully analyzed the publications of university professors and students in Taiwan during the years of political ferment. I also corresponded extensively with many participants, inquiring into a number of points that needed clarification. In December 1973-January 1974, I again visited Taiwan and interviewed many people involved in the activities related in this study. Their encouragement and support contributed substantially to this work.

I would like to express my thanks to Professors A. Doak Barnett of the Brookings Institution, Robert Scalapino of the University of California, and Allen Whiting, Rhoads Murphey, and Michel Oksenberg of the University of Michigan for reading the draft of this manuscript and making helpful comments. I would also like to thank Mrs. Sharon Goss and my colleagues Paul Morman and Frederick Bartle at the New York State University College at Oswego for their editorial help in preparing this manuscript for publication.

Mab Huang
Oswego, New York
February 1976

PROFILE OF PROMINENT PARTICIPANTS

Chang Ching-hang (also Chun-hung), a political scientist trained at
National Taiwan University, was born in the late 1930s in
Nantow, Taiwan, the son of a primary school teacher. From the
[illegible]
ment. In October 1971, he was chosen by the young intellectual group to draft a program for political reforms. In late
1972, he was invited by the State Department of the United
States to visit this country. Upon his return he was implicated
in the case of Professor Chen Ku-ying and others and was
forced to resign from his party post. He ran for a seat on
the City Council of Taipei in late 1973 and was defeated by a
narrow margin.

Chen Ku-ying, a promising philosopher and favored disciple of the
late Professor Yin Hai-kuang, was born in Fukien, China, in
1935. He taught for many years at National Taiwan University
and was known for his studies of Laotse and the Life of Jesus,
among other works. A young man of high intelligence, elo-
quence, and poetic touch, he was adored by his students.
During 1971-1972, he passionately championed human rights,
particularly the right of students to speak their mind. In
April 1972, his position on the student movement was severely
attacked. In July-August 1972, he toured the United States
and came into contact with intellectual groups of different
political persuasions. When he returned to Taiwan, he participated actively in the debate on nationalism then going on
and severely criticized Western liberalism. In March 1973,
he was detained for twenty-four hours by the Taiwan Garrison
Command on a charge of involvement in a pro-Communist
"reading club." He was dismissed from the university after
this incident.

ix

Chen Shao-ting, born in Ping-tung, Taiwan, in the early 1930s, was a prominent political scientist educated at National Taiwan University. He has many scholarly works to his credit, including On Totalitarianism, The Meaning of the Twentieth Century, and On Culture and Politics. Possibly because a high school teacher of his had been convicted as a Communist spy, he was suspect to the authorities and in danger of being jailed. Due to this political liability, he was not able to secure a position at National Taiwan University. For years, he lived in Tainan City and worked for Professor Morton Fried of Columbia University as a research associate. A leading member of the Ta-hsueh tsa-chih she, he was particularly well-known during 1971-1972 for demanding "comprehensive reelection" of the three bodies of the people's representatives at the national level.

Chu Hungdah, a well-known scholar in international law, was born in Fukien, China, in the late 1930s. Educated at National Taiwan University and Harvard University, he has been a research associate at Harvard Law School. In the academic year 1971-1972, he was a visiting professor at National Chengchi University. Given his cordial relationship with the Nationalist Party leadership, he played a significant role in the early phase of the ferment for political reforms.

Hu Fu, an expert in constitutional law and political parties, was born in Kiangsu, China, in the early 1930s into a wealthy family that had close ties with the Nationalist Party. Educated at National Taiwan University and Emory University in Georgia, he returned in the early 1960s to teach at the former while serving in an important administrative position at the Academia Sinica. A leading member of the Szu-yu yen she, he was accused of participating in a conspiracy to use that group to take over the Academia Sinica in the service of Professor John K. Fairbank and indirectly of the Chinese Communists. His study of the Control Yuan, documenting the predominant influence of the ruling party in that body, was censured by the Nationalist Party as slander. In 1969, he spent a year in the United States as a visiting scholar at Yale University. In 1971-1972, he was known for his exposition of democracy and human rights.

Wang Shao-po, an instructor in philosophy at National Taiwan University and an eloquent champion of social justice in the early 1970s, was born in Fukien, China, in the late 1930s. His father was a military officer of the Nationalist army; his mother, convicted as a Communist spy, was executed by the authorities when he was a young child. Brought up by his

[illegible — text obscured]

department in 1974.

Yang Kuo-shu, a pioneering scholar in the studies of Chinese national character and student attitudes, was educated at National Taiwan University and the University of Illinois. He was born in Shangtung, China, in the early 1930s. Known for his integrity, fairness, and ability to work with different groups, he played a crucial role in the ferment for political reforms. The success of the Ta-hsueh tsa-chih was to a substantial degree attributable to his talents, patience, and hard work.

I. DIPLOMATIC SETBACKS

The intellectual ferment for political reforms came unexpectedly to Taiwan in the years 1971-1973. During the 1960s, diverse groups of intellectuals had taken to arguing the need for new knowl-

[illegible faded text]

Young intellectuals moved into the political arena for the first time in two decades.

In a sense, it was paradoxical that young university professors and students took to agitation for political reforms when the Republic of China on Taiwan was fighting for survival as an autonomous political entity; yet, on closer examination, there was a logic to what took place in the years 1971-1973. It was precisely because diplomatic setbacks had weakened the authority of the ruling party and the government that the criticisms of the intellectuals had to be acknowledged and their ferment for political reforms accommodated. Given the serious challenge facing the nation as they saw it, the intellectuals summoned their courage to speak of the ills of society and play the role of instigators of political reforms.

For the preceding two decades, since Chiang Kai-shek and the Nationalist Party had withdrawn from the mainland, the ruling party and government had governed Taiwan with a firm hand. With aid and support from the United States and the use of security police, particularly in the early 1950s, the Republic of China had survived both the threat that Peking would liberate Taiwan by force and the challenge of the Taiwanese Independence Movement.[2] In Taiwan Chiang Kai-shek and his party ruled supreme. Politics were conducted in a highly autocratic style, with the ultimate power to make decisions on a wide range of issues reserved for the General Director of the ruling party.[3]

1

The only time Chiang Kai-shek's rule had been seriously challenged was when Lei Chen and his supporters moved to organize an opposition party in the late 1950s and early 1960s.[4] Lei Chen, a former high-ranking official of the Nationalist Party and the publisher of the Tzu-yu chung-kuo [Free China fortnightly] joined forces with a number of well-known intellectuals and prominent Taiwanese politicians and community leaders in a concerted effort to oppose the ruling party. Their protest against the abuse of power by the ruling party and government, against manipulation of elections and denial of political participation, apparently appealed to many sectors of the society. However, before long the ruling party decided to suppress the embryonic opposition party. In September 1960, Lei Chen was arrested and convicted by the military court for protecting an ex-Communist agent on the Tzu-yu chung-kuo staff and was sentenced to ten years in jail. The journal was closed down, and the opposition party did not see the light of day.

It can be taken as an indication of the tight control exercised by the ruling party and government that the crackdown on Lei Chen and his embryonic party did not provoke any substantial protest from the intellectual community or society in general. Hu Shih, the eminent philosopher, was reputed to have encouraged the formation of an opposition party and agreed to serve as its advisor; yet when the crisis came, he remained silent. A few newspapers and journals in Taiwan and Hong Kong did condemn the government. So did a journal published by a group of Chinese intellectuals in New York City.[5] The protest, however, was as ineffective as it was muted. From the viewpoint of the ruling party, the crisis was handled effectively, if awkwardly.

During the sixties the intellectuals chafed under a straitjacket. Any "heretical" opinions were not tolerated. Many a well-known professor and young intellectual paid a high price for criticizing the Nationalist Party and the government; they were harassed, kept under surveillance, and persecuted. Yin Hai-kwong, a philosophy professor at National Taiwan University and a close friend of Lei Chen and Hu Shih, was driven from the university and denied the right to give public lectures. His book, Reappraisal of Cultural Change in Modern China (in Chinese), was proscribed. Until his premature death due to cancer, he held fast to liberalism and refused to compromise with the government, setting an example of integrity and courage.[6] Po Yang, a popular anti-Communist journalist and literary writer, was accused of insulting the dignity of the head of state as well as of having been a Communist agent in 1949. He was arrested in March 1969 and sentenced by a military court to imprisonment.[7] Li Ao, the young historian and counter-culture youth hero in Taiwan, was arrested and jailed in April 1971 after years of harassment.[8] The journal Wen-hsing tsa-chi, with

these incidents suffice to illustrate the plight of intellectuals in Taiwan.

From the perspective of the ruling party and government, the motivations for keeping the intellectuals under control are not difficult to ascertain. Both ideology and self-interest played a part. Chiang Kai-shek and many Nationalist leaders had never really been sympathetic to liberalism, which since the May Fourth Movement had become a dormant yet potential political force in China.[11] They tended to equate liberalism with selfishness and lack of discipline, regarding it as an alien ideology not suitable for China. Worse still, they saw liberalism as a Trojan horse employed by the Chinese Communists for the destruction of traditional culture. To their discomfort, many of the intellectuals critical of the ruling party and government in Taiwan, such as Yin Hai-kwong and Li Ao, were profoundly influenced by the spirit of the May Fourth Movement. Furthermore, the Chinese intellectuals had always deemed themselves, as they still do, the conscience of society and the spokesmen of the people; and they were accepted as such. Though they did not have power, their authority could not be denied; thus, they were always a threat to the ruling elite. Tension between the ruling elite and the intellectuals, if subdued, was almost inevitable, awaiting the opportune time to erupt.

Despite this tight control, Taiwan enjoyed a degree of political stability and prosperity.[12] Yet beneath the economic prosperity and progress lurked many serious problems, as the young intellectuals would discover in the early seventies.[13] The entrepreneur class was satisfied, given the rapid development of capitalist enterprises and its support from the government. But the rank and file government functionaries, the military personnel, and in particular the peasantry and laboring class had not shared in the prosperity of the society to any equitable degree. Moreover, by the early seventies the villages were no longer prosperous, as they had been for a period of time after the Land Reform in the early fifties; nor were cities equal to the task of absorbing and caring for the young and unskilled laborers coming from the countryside.

Equally vital in the development of Taiwan, political stability was turning into political stagnation. Chiang Kai-shek and the party leadership, growing old and wedded to old ideas, held on to power. While there were indeed indications that Chiang Ching-kuo was prepared to take over the government, and that he and his close associates did not see eye to eye on many issues with elder party leaders, it was clear that Chiang Ching-kuo was determined to defer to his father in all crucial policy matters, patiently waiting for his turn. The problem of elite circulation was particularly serious. The National Assembly, the Legislative Yuan, and the Control Yuan, all elected in 1947 when the Nationalist Party and government were still in control of the mainland, faced depletion and physical weakness in their membership. Of the 2,961 National Assembly members elected in 1947, only 1,393 were still serving in 1971; of the 759 members of the Legislative Yuan, 434 remained; while in the Control Yuan membership declined from 180 in 1949 to 69 in April 1971.[14] Furthermore, due to old age and ill health, many of the people's representatives still serving simply could not perform their tasks. In 1971, the average age of the National Assembly's membership was 65; in 1970, the average age of the Legislative Yuan's membership was 65, while that of the Control Yuan was over 70.[15] Yet a solution proved to be extremely difficult. Concerned with the issue of legitimacy, i.e., its claim to be the only government of China, and desiring to retain the support of the people's representatives at the national level, the ruling party and government were not prepared to take any drastic measures.

After long deliberation and planning, a compromise was decided upon. The National Assembly in 1966 amended the Constitution to authorize President Chiang to hold a supplementary election of the three bodies. The election was duly held in December 1969 in

Taipei City and Taiwan Province. Altogether, fifteen new members were elected to the National Assembly, eleven to the Legislative Yuan, and two to the Control Yuan. All the new members were native Taiwanese.[16] This first supplementary election, salutary as it might be in furthering political participation, did not create a broader power base. Given the size of the three organs and the control exercised by the ruling party, the newly elected people's representatives could not make much of a

fields of economic and financial affairs. Moreover, on the provincial level, the governor was appointed by the central government which for years had chosen a military man, thus limiting the opportunities of native Taiwanese civilian politicians. Tight control of local elections of Provincial Assembly members, city majors, city councilmen, hsien magistrates, and hsien councilmen by the ruling party, and recurring complaints of election fraud and manipulation also made for political tension.

During the early 1970s, the series of diplomatic setbacks noted earlier began to weaken the government's position. After decades of political stability, economic prosperity, and international recognition, the survival of the government of the Republic of China in Taiwan as an autonomous political entity was threatened. The first serious challenge facing the ruling party and government in Taiwan was the issue of the Tiao-yu-tai Islets,[18] a cluster of rock girt islands and lonely reefs lying some 120 miles northeast of Taiwan and 570 miles southwest of Japan. Since the end of the second World War, the islets had been occupied and administered by the United States as part of Okinawa. For centuries these islets served primarily as a refuge for Chinese fishermen, and until recently Chinese fishermen had still used them. However, with the discovery of oil deposits around the islets reported by the Economic Commission of Asia and the Far East in 1968-69, China, Taiwan, and Japan immediately became entangled in a jurisdictional dispute. On August 10, 1970, in a speech before the House of

Councillors, the Japanese Foreign Minister Aichi unilaterally claimed the islets. A month later, Japan again reiterated its position, indicating that the Japanese government would decline to engage in any discussion on the issue of the islets' sovereignty.

These statements were followed by activity. On September 15, the police of Okinawa pulled down the national flag of the Republic of China on the islets. The next day, Chinese fishermen from Taiwan working near the islets were driven away by two Japanese naval vessels. And a few days later, it was reported that the Japanese government intended to allocate 300,000 yen to the government of Okinawa for the purpose of operating a weather bureau. Furthermore, the United States appeared to take a position favoring Japan. In a statement issued by the Department of State on September 10, 1970, the United States suggested that Okinawa would be restored to Japan in accord with the agreement between President Nixon and Premier Sato and that disposition of the Tiao-yu-tai Islets should be left to the negotiations of the nations concerned. Again on April 9, 1971, the U.S. Department of State made it clear that the islets would be returned to Japan in 1972 with the Okinawa Islands.

Peking, after having supported the Japanese claim to Okinawa since the late 1950s, issued a statement on December 4, 1970, claiming that the Tiao-yu-tai Islets were part of Taiwan and thus a part of China.

When the dispute over the islets began, the government of the Republic of China in Taiwan acted cautiously. On July 17, 1969, the government claimed the right to use natural resources beyond its territorial sea. In the same month, the Chinese Petroleum Company signed a contract with American companies for the exploration of oil deposits around the islets. In September 1971, the government reiterated its claim to the islets; it took the position that Japan was not a legitimate negotiator, citing the fact that both the Okinawa Islands and the Tiao-yu-tai Islets were still under the administrative control of the United States. However, it indicated that, as an ally, the government would not refuse to discuss informally with Japan the issues involved. Moreover, the government had, through a private organization, the Committee for the Promotion of Sino-Japanese Cooperation, participated in a meeting held in November 1970 in Tokyo. As a result, Japan, Taiwan, and South Korea agreed to exploit jointly the natural resources of the sea, and a Joint Committee for Ocean Development Research was set up. This move, however, was not disclosed to the public until March 1971; when reference was made to it, the spokesman insisted that none of the issues regarding the sovereignty of the islets were discussed at the meeting.[19]

[illegible] pute.[20] The reaction was, not unexpectedly, most violent among intellectuals in Taiwan and abroad. The posture taken by the government toward Japan and, to a lesser degree, toward the United States was seen as a sign of weakness and betrayal of national interest.

In late 1970, a group of young students in Hong Kong issued a statement condemning Japanese aggression and urged Chinese throughout the world to unite and defend the islets. In the early part of November 1970, Chinese students at Princeton and the University of Wisconsin, led by Li Teh-yu, Hu Po-kai and others, began to hold meetings on how to handle the dispute. A pamphlet on Tiao-yu-tai affairs was issued. On December 19, Chinese students at Princeton University decided on a demonstration, heralding the Protect Tiao-yu-tai Movement in the United States and Taiwan. Soon students in the New York City area, Chicago, and Seattle joined in. "Protect Tiao-yu-tai Islets" groups were established in many an American city and university; meetings were held, pamphlets were published, and a coordination network was set up. On January 29 and 30, 1971, Chinese intellectuals and university students demonstrated in six American cities: New York, Washington, D. C., Chicago, Seattle, San Francisco, and Los Angeles, with 2,000 to 3,000 persons taking part. In New York City alone, about 1,000 Chinese demonstrated at the United Nations plaza. They came from Boston, New Haven, Pennsylvania, New Jersey, and New York and included Chinese students from Taiwan, Hong Kong, and Malaysia as well as American-born Chinese. The demonstration was fairly orderly. Participants sang and distributed pamphlets as they moved along. It was a spontaneous patriotic movement, reminiscent of the May Fourth Movement some sixty years before, and not yet divided by the ideological cleavage that was soon to come. The Yi-ho-chuan (Boxers), the self-styled Maoist group in Chinatown, New York City, also participated in the demonstration, though their influence was rather limited. They attempted to distribute pamphlets of their own but were prevented from doing so. The only group that did not take part was the Formosan Independence Movement, probably because they were faced with a dilemma: given their tie with Japan, they could find it embarrassing to demonstrate against Japanese foreign policy.[21]

On April 10, 1971, in the wake of the American declaration of intent to turn over to Japan in 1972 administrative right to the Tiao-yu-tai Islets, about 2,500 Chinese intellectuals and students in the United States came to Washington, D. C., and staged a demonstration against the policy of the United States and Japan.[22] While university students took to the streets, older Chinese intellectuals in the United States also contributed their share to the momentum. On March 19, 1971, some 500 well-known scholars in the United States wrote to President Chiang urging him to "stand firm on the issue of Tiao-yu-tai and resist the new aggression of Japan." Three days later, the President replied that he would definitely do so and thanked them for their patriotism.[23]

Faced with pressure from the Chinese intellectual community in the United States to take a firm position on the Tiao-yu-tai dispute, the government of the Republic of China in Taiwan responded defensively. Initially Chung-yang jih-pao, the organ of the Nationalist Party, reporting on the demonstrations in the United States, suggested that the Chinese students abroad supported the government's position; yet beneath the surface there was a sense of nervousness. An editorial on February 5 asserted that Japan was not faced with the problem of militarism, and any attack on the revival of Japanese militarism would be seen as part of a Chinese Communist plot to divide the anti-Communist camp.[24] Though this editorial did not refer to the Tiao-yu-tai movement, Chinese students in the United States were enraged by the implicit accusation that the movement was instigated or controlled by the Chinese Communists. In addition, rumors circulated in the United States that the Embassy in Washington, D. C., and Consulate Generals in many

American cities had done their best to discourage the demonstrations, to divide the Chinese groups, and in some cases, to threaten or rough up individual participants in the movement.

Apparently the embassy and diplomats of the Republic of China in the United States were obsessed with fear that the Chinese Com-

[illegible text]

ally the movement was divided by ideological cleavage.[26] Those who supported Peking urged unification of China under Communist rule; those who supported the Nationalist Party organized themselves into the "Patriotic Anti-Communist Alliance"; and many Chinese professionals and students simply withdrew from any further participation.

In Taiwan, intellectuals and university students were also provoked by the dispute. As early as November 1970, a group of overseas Chinese students at National Taiwan University made plans to demonstrate in front of the Japanese Embassy; however, given the conciliatory position of the government, they were dissuaded by university authorities from doing so.[27] In April 1971, ninety-three university professors, students, and young men and women working in government and business issued a statement asserting that the Tiao-yu-tai Islets were part of China and professing support of the government in any measure it took to protect sovereignty.[28] Many of the signatories of this statement, including Professors Hungdah Chiu, Chen Ku-ying, Yang Kuo-shu, Mr. Chen Shao-ting, Mr. Chang Shao-wen, Mr. Chang Ching-hang and others, were later to play a crucial part in the ferment for political reforms.

Following the news on April 9, 1971, of United States intent to turn over the islets to Japan and after demonstrations by Chinese intellectuals in America, the university students could no longer be controlled. On April 12 and 13, 1971, posters protesting Japanese aggression and American acquiescence began to appear en masse at the campus of National Taiwan University, National Chengchi University, and National Normal University, all in Taipei.[29] Meetings were held and Committees for the Protection of the Tiao-yu-tai Islets were set up. On April 15 and 16, wave after wave of demonstrations took place. On April 14, about 100 overseas Chinese students, primarily from National Taiwan University, demonstrated at the Embassy of Japan. About 1,000 overseas Chinese students from the three universities demonstrated in front of the United States Embassy on the 15th, delivering a letter of protest; on the 16th, ten delegates from National Taiwan University delivered a letter of protest signed by 2,500 students to the American Embassy and presented themselves at the Embassy of Japan.

At National Normal University, about 100 overseas students staged a sit-down strike on April 14; on the 17th, 4,000 students held a meeting in the stadium and staged a demonstration on the campus; and following that, about 2,000 students signed a protest with their blood. At National Chengchi University, against the wishes of the authorities, a demonstration was staged on the 13th; a delegation of twelve students also met with the American Ambassador to deliver their protest on the 14th and was received by a high-ranking official in the Japanese Embassy.

Through these April days of protest and demonstration, the overseas Chinese students attending universities apparently took the lead. This was in part because, as students abroad, they were given more freedom of action by the government; their emotional response could be explained by the fact that, living abroad, particularly in Hong Kong and Southeast Asia, they were more sensitive to humiliation and the issue of national sovereignty.

The government, it should be noted, was opposed to demonstrations. It made the utmost effort to dissuade the students from staging demonstrations, and when this was not possible, to control them so that they would not embarrass the government. The degree to which the press in Taiwan was strenuously controlled by the government was also clearly demonstrated through these days of demonstrations. Reports on student activities were few and clearly downplayed. Students at National Normal University were so angered by the news coverage that they urged a boycott of the newspapers, leading to a meeting between the students and the press on the 17th. Although the journalists did their best to explain why they did not play a more active role, they failed to convince the students.

In June 1971, angered by the "agreement" between the United States and Japan on the transfer of administration rights over the Tiao-yu-tai Islets, the students at National Taiwan University again staged a massive demonstration.[30] On June 14, posters appeared en masse on the campus. The next day the Committee for the Protection of the Tiao-yu-tai Islets called for demonstrations. The

patriots" was highly emotional and nationalistic. It referred to the anti-Japanese war, the occupation of Taiwan by Japan, and imperial encroachment on China in the past hundred years, and urged the Chinese to rise up in defense of national sovereignty. The letters to the governments of the United States and Japan were equally passionate and the points were sharply made. In the former, the American government was accused of committing in Asia an act akin to the Munich conspiracy; in the latter, Japan was warned against again forcing the Chinese nation to war. The demonstration took place on June 17, with more than one thousand students participating. To maintain order, selected students and government security officials cordoned off the American Embassy before the group arrived. Though highly emotional, the demonstrators were fairly well-disciplined. Citizens in the streets applauded them when they arrived, the letter to the United States government was read aloud, and three students, Hung San-hsiang, Chang Tai-hsiang, and Chen Pei-chien went into the embassy to deliver it. while outside students shouted slogans: "Protect the Tiao-yu-tai Islets"; "The Tiao-yu-tai Islets belong to us"; "Down with the Japanese and U.S. conspiracy." The group then moved on to the Japanese Embassy. Many students shouted, "Japanese devils get out." Again, Chang Tai-hsiang read aloud the letter of protest and went inside the embassy to deliver it. By noon the demonstration was over.

In this demonstration the Ta-hsueh tsa-chih journal began to play a more definite role. Its editorial formally protested the American and Japanese positions on the Tiao-yu-tai Islets; any agreement on Okinawa between Japan and the United States would be regarded as null and void. Furthermore, a new note was sounded. Urging a thorough self-examination regarding the plight of the nation, it insisted that only a thorough reform could save the nation.

> What we refer to as political reforms are not only im-
> provements in administrative efficiency; they are basic
> reforms of the political structure. We always hold the
> view that only if internal politics were healthy and mod-
> ern could we establish a sound international position and
> provide a strong basis for success in diplomacy. Based
> on this belief, we with a heavy heart, urge the govern-
> ment authorities . . . to thoroughly wipe out any and
> all accumulated defects, use new men of talent, cour-
> age, and knowledge, as well as provide opportunity for
> fair competition for all so that we could together create
> modern institutions.[31]

When summer recess came and students left the universities, the "Protect Tiao-yu-tai Movement" subsided. Yet less than a month later, the government of the Republic of China on Taiwan was faced with a most serious challenge when President Nixon announced on July 16 that he would visit China to seek normalization of relations. Even though he took pains to emphasize that the "action will not be at the expense of our old friends," apparently referring to the government of Taiwan, the news inevitably produced a serious shock.[32] To be sure there had been signs that the United States was moving towards a more conciliatory position towards Peking, but Nixon's decision was seen as a sudden move, heralding serious consequences. The Chinese Ambassador to the United States delivered a strong protest note to the U.S. Department of State denouncing the Nixon visit as a "shady deal"; Deputy Foreign Minister Yang Hsi-kun in Taipei summoned the American Ambassador to deliver a protest note; the Vice-President also made a statement, asserting that the deceit practiced by the Chinese Communists would be refuted by facts and the forces of truth and justice would ultimately triumph.[33]

The Nationalist Party and governmental officials were dismayed; relations between the United States and Taiwan became more formal and cool, if correct.[34] However, there was no sense of panic; for the party and government were assured that the United States would meet its treaty obligation. The posture of the government was that, while the Republic of China had been wronged, it would persist in its course of truth and justice and, through self-reliance, survive the crisis and prosper. Taking a leaf from a speech given by President Chiang in June 1971,[35] the slogan of "Don't be disquieted in times of adverse change. Remain firm with dignity. Be self-

support of the United States and Japan, as well as some African and Latin American nations, the government hoped that it could weather the crisis in 1971. Thus, the government did not prepare the people for what was to come to pass. Likewise, the newspapers day after day stressed the support the Republic of China enjoyed in the world arena and professed the conviction that any move to expel it from the United Nations would be defeated. During this period, a new slogan on posters and banners appeared in the streets of Taipei. It read, "Resolutely resist the attempt of the Peking bandit regime to sneak into the U. N."[37]

At the United Nations General Assembly, a complicated maneuver was going on. The United States adopted the position that expulsion of the delegate of the Republic of China should be treated as "an important issue," and the Japanese government was persuaded to co-sponsor an American proposal to seat both Peking and Taipei. Yet in a sense, as pointed out by critics of American policy, the American support of Taipei was half-heartedly and clumsily executed. While the General Assembly was meeting, Kissinger was visiting in Peking. This, many felt, gave the impression that the United States was not serious in its backing of the Republic of China.[38] After weeks of lobbying by the American delegate, the United States proposal was defeated by a four-vote margin (55 to 59, with 15 abstentions). At that point Foreign Minister Chow Shu-kai criticized the United Nations for "flagrant violation of the Charter" and withdrew from the General Assembly. Immediately after that, the General Assembly voted (76 to 35, with 17 abstentions) to "expel forthwith the representatives of Chiang Kai-shek from the place which they unlawfully occupy at the United Nations."[39]

In Taipei the government reacted rather calmly. President Chiang in his "Letter to Our Compatriots," denounced the vote of the General Assembly as unlawful and predicted the self-destruction of the United Nations.[40] This theme was echoed again and again by government officials. There was a sense of frustration, indignation, and apprehension in the air. University campuses, unexpectedly, were quiet. A demonstration outside the U.S. Embassy was peaceful and well-disciplined. During the evening news, many citizens interviewed on the Taiwan Television Network were angry and bitter, accusing Nixon of betrayal. University students interviewed by the network on different campuses, however, tended to react somewhat differently. They were more critical of the government and gave more thought to the future. Many of them expressed the belief that only through political reforms could Taiwan face the future with any sense of confidence.[41] By this time, it need be noted, the intellectuals grouped around the Ta-hsueh tsa-chih had already published their statement, heralding the political reform movement.[42]

From the fall of 1971 on, the position of the Republic of China in the international arena deteriorated rapidly. Amid signs that Peking was working diligently to isolate Taiwan, Nixon's visit in February 1972 was anxiously awaited by the government and people in Taiwan. However, while the United States was going through a new wave of enthusiasm about China and things Chinese at the time of President Nixon's visit, the news of his arrival and his discussions with Mao Tse-tung and Premier Chou En-lai were played down in Taiwan. Reports from Peking by American newspapermen and television crews were entirely blacked out. It was rumored in Taipei that Vice-President C. K. Yen and Chiang Ching-kuo had made arrangements with the television network for a private view of Nixon's visit; but the intellectual community in Taiwan could only rely on American journals such as Time, Newsweek, and U.S. News and World Report for its information, while the masses depended on Chinese newspapers from Hong Kong. Thirst for information was such that for a few days a brisk market existed for those Hong Kong newspapers sympathetic to the government on Taiwan and permitted to circulate.[43] Nevertheless, the tone of reaction was set by Chiang Kai-shek. Significantly, in his opening speech to the

National Assembly in Taipei, he did not refer to the Nixon visit. He asserted that the Chinese Communist regime had failed to maintain effective control over the mainland, citing the purges of Liu Shao-chi and Lin Piao, and warned against the illusion that a balance of power scheme would be conducive to world peace.[44]

In May 1972, before the transfer of the Tiao-yu-tai Islets to Japan, the Foreign Ministry again reasserted the sovereignty of the Republic of China over the islets and protested the impending transfer.[47] University students, on the whole, were quiet. The Protect Tiao-yu-tai Movement had exhausted itself,[48] partly due to frustration and partly because students' attentions were focusing on agitation for basic political reforms. The only protest took place at National Taiwan University where Mr. Wang Hu-su, president of the Student Association and an active participant in the movement, led a few students in a hunger strike on May 15, the day the Tiao-yu-tai Islets were transferred to Japan. He and his friends chained themselves to the Fu Ssu-lien Bell Tower on campus. It was a stormy day and the downpour must have added a sense of drama. Reportedly the government was prepared to send in plain-clothes police to arrest them. Fearing provocation, the university spent long hours in telephone consultations and maneuverings and finally succeeded in dissuading the government from action while they persuaded Mr. Wang and his friends to disperse.[49] Since university students on other campuses failed to join in, the gallant act of Mr. Wang and his friends at National Taiwan University was a mere symbol of defiance and frustration.

During the summer and fall of 1972, the position of the Republic of China in the world arena continued to worsen. Many countries either recognized Peking, compelling a severance of ties with Taipei, or moved towards establishing diplomatic relations with the

People's Republic of China. The crucial issue, however, was whether Japan would move to recognize Peking. Since the Nixon visit to China, there were signs that Japan was reappraising its policy towards China, and pressure within Japan to change its course were mounting rapidly. The government on Taiwan could only hope to maintain its status quo.

The feeling towards Japan was extremely complicated. On the one hand, the ruling party and government hoped that, given the historical tie and President Chiang's generous treatment of Japan in the postwar years, Japanese politicians would be grateful and supportive of the government on Taiwan; on the other hand, they realized that Taiwan relied heavily on Japan both diplomatically and economically and could not risk a break with Japan. Within the intellectual community, opinion was divided. For many professors and university students, particularly those from mainland China, a residual sense of antagonism, if not hatred, toward Japan could still be discerned. In addition, Japanese influence on many aspects of life in Taiwan was adding insult to injury. Professor Kao Chun, an art historian, went so far as to argue that a voluntary army should be mobilized to occupy Tokyo, thus forcing Japan to give in.[50] Many scholars and professionals, however, tended to be more sober in their views and more tolerant of the Japanese position on Taiwan.

In contrast to reactions against the American rapprochement with Peking, reaction against a similar move by the Tanaka government of Japan was emotional and bitter. A sense of betrayal was shared by the government and society at large. When the Nixon-Tanaka Communique was issued, and it was clear that Premier Tanaka was planning to visit Peking, the government indicated intense disapproval. On September 3, the Foreign Ministry commented on the Communique and protested the move, arguing that the Tanaka visit would only produce greater tensions in Asia and the Pacific areas.[51] The editorial of the Chung-yang jih-pao also pointed out that such a "conspiracy" between the Tanaka government and the Chinese Communists was an act of betrayal of trust and justice and would definitely impair the security of Asian nations.[52] On September 12, through the initiative of the government, more than 8,000 university and college professors made public a statement protesting Japanese policy, urging the Chinese people to rise up and accept the challenge.[53] Mr. Ku Cheng-kang, chief delegate of the Republic of China to the Asian Parliamentarian meeting in Japan, also took advantage of his meeting with Tanaka to warn him of the dire consequences of establishing diplomatic relations with mainland China. Premier Tanaka was noncommittal in his reply while indicating he still supported the Asian Parliamentarian group.[54] But these open pressures and persuasions, as well as behind-the-scene maneuvers

try in Taipei declared that any agreement between Peking and Tokyo would be considered null and void.[58] On September 30, 1972, the day following the establishment of diplomatic relations between China and Japan, Taiwan announced the severance of relations with Japan, denouncing the accord as a "perfidious act."[59] On September 25, heavy security was imposed in Taipei and the Japanese Embassy was cordoned off, though no demonstration was staged.[60] Chinese doctors and nurses in Keeling City burned about $5,000 worth of Japanese medicine and declared a boycott against Japanese goods;[61] the next day, Tanaka photos were burned in protest by university students.[62]

Japan's new China policy also provoked a debate on nationalism among intellectuals.[63] Within the span of one week, on December 4 and again on December 11, 1972, the Tai-ta Lun-tan-she, a student organization at National Taiwan University, sponsored two forums on nationalism. Chen Yu-ching, newly appointed director of the Committee on Overseas Affairs of the ruling party, Professor Chen Ku-ying, Professor Wang Shao-po, and Professor Wang Wen-hsing, among others, spoke at the first forum. Briefly, Mr. Chen Yu-ching asserted that China must be unified; yet the crucial issue was how and for what. He argued forcefully that unification was meaningful only if China were unified as a free and democratic nation. Identity with Chinese culture, Chinese spirit, and Chinese ways of life, unification, and national independence, he stated, should be goals. "But we cannot identify with the Communist regime in mainland China; we should identify with the China that defends and promotes Chinese culture and spirit. And our government has already been making efforts in this direction," he said. Professor Wang Wen-hsing took a somewhat different position. As a novelist and literary critic, he was skeptical of excessive nationalism in the political arena and absolutely repudiated it in art and literature. It was left for Professors Chen Ku-ying and Wang Shao-po to argue the case of militant nationalism. Both condemned the encroachment of the imperialist nations, in particular the economic aggression and cultural influence of the United States and Japan. Intellectuals in Taiwan were taken to task. They were accused of not speaking out on behalf of society because of satisfaction with their status. Given the influence of economic development and Western culture, the country had succumbed to capitalist values, they argued. As Professor Chen Ku-ying put it, "Many people say that Taiwan is a society of pluralist values; in my writings, I had also dreamed of making Taiwan an open society of pluralist values. In fact, we in Taiwan have accepted the value system of the capitalist society; (we can hardly speak) of pluralist values."[64] This condemnation, coming from Professor Chen at this time, was indeed ironic. For more than anyone else, in the previous years of political ferment, he had the reputation of being a staunch liberal, the voice for freedom, democracy and social justice. His shifting of position, which was as dismaying to many of his colleagues as it was provoking to the government, says much about the minds of intellectuals in time of crisis.

Immediately following this forum, students of National Taiwan University were drawn into the debate. Some attacked Professors Chen and Wang Shao-po as "New Boxers," emotional in their anti-imperialist campaign, oblivious to the threat posed by Communism, and ready to sacrifice freedom and democracy in curing what they saw as the ills of the society.[65] Others defended them with equal passion.[66] Accusations and counteraccusations were exchanged; the debate soon took a turn toward personal attacks and ended on a desultory note. Like the hunger strike by Mr. Wang Hu-su and his friends at the Fu Ssu-lien Bell Tower, this debate was a manifestation of impotence and frustration in the face of political reality.

In summation, the diplomatic setbacks sustained by the government in the early 1970s provoked the young intellectuals in Taiwan to enter the political arena. As the crisis weakened the authorities of the ruling party and government, the activities of the young university professors and students were to a greater degree tolerated.

To defend national sovereignty, particularly sovereignty over the Tiao-yu-tai Islets, the university professors and students held forums, made speeches, wrote petitions, and organized demonstrations. They were, however, destined to be frustrated by political reality. The government on Taiwan took a conciliatory position on the dispute; and the American and Japanese governments were not

II. INTELLECTUAL FERMENT FOR POLITICAL REFORMS

It was but a short step from the Protect Tiao-yu-tai Movement to the ferment for political reforms. Though the circumstances were different, the development was reminiscent of the May Fourth Movement some sixty years before.[1] In both incidents, [illegible]

[illegible] urged youth to dare to speak their minds, Professors Chen Ku-ying and Liu Fu-chen, both of the Philosophy Department at National Taiwan University, and Mr. Chang Shao-wen, of the Republic of China branch of the International Junior Chamber of Commerce, wrote an open letter to Chiang Ching-kuo. They explained why the youth dared not speak their minds and what should be done to remedy the situation. As they saw it, youth dared not speak because they felt they were not trusted by the government and that any criticism of the party and government would be construed as hostile, as some sort of "ideological deviation." Given the tight control by the security police, any record of "ideological deviation" would haunt a youth, hurting his career chances. They suggested that Chiang Ching-kuo should seek an opportunity himself to talk with and listen to those intellectuals who are "patriotic and dare speak the truth." Furthermore, they felt he should provide opportunities for meetings with university student groups, so that young people could freely state their views. Finally, if any youth had been blacklisted by the public security organs for what they supposedly had said, they should be given a chance to explain and defend themselves; only thus, they concluded in their letter, could youth dare to speak.[2]

Simultaneous with the publication of this letter, a group of articles appeared in the <u>Ta-hsueh tsa-chih</u> taking a more critical view of politics and society. Among them, four articles were particularly noteworthy. Writing on toleration, Professor Chen Ku-ying spoke movingly on behalf of human rights and freedom of speech and thought. Long periods of spiritual fetters and suppression of freedom of speech and thought, he warned, must lead to the stagnation of scholarship, stifling of personality development, and withering of the forces of life. Condemning arbitrary use of power by the security police and control of university students by the authorities, he urged that any problem relating to "security measures" or "ideological deviation" must be handled in accordance with legal procedures and that government and university authorities must nurture students and encourage their participation in public affairs. [3]

Mr. Chen Shao-ting argued forcefully for academic freedom, for in his view, the promotion of academic freedom was not only compatible with "national security" but also provided a source of knowledge needed for defending the security of the nation. [4] Mr. Chang Ching-hang, dwelling on obstacles to modernization, proposed that instead of "seeking progress in stability," which had been the guiding policy for the past two decades, the policy should be one of "seeking long-term stability in progress." A fair and effective "personnel system," he argued, should be "institutionalized." For given the peculiar historical background which had contributed to a sense of antagonism between mainlanders and native Taiwanese, equality of opportunity should be encouraged so that regional differences would not serve as a blockade to modernization. [5] The antagonism between mainlanders and native Taiwanese, it should be noted, had been a taboo for some two decades; now that it was being openly discussed, one of the most cherished myths of the ruling elite was vigorously challenged.

Mr. Shao Hsiang-feng, a researcher at the Ministry of Economic Affairs, in his discussion of economic development in Taiwan, also took to task the often proclaimed "economic miracle." Arguing that with the economic base left by the Japanese and aid from the United States, economic development on Taiwan was nothing to be proud of. The issue, as he saw it, was whether Taiwan would develop along the capitalist path, favoring the few at the expense of the many, or whether emphasis should be placed on fair distribution of social wealth. To resolve the problem, he urged for popular participation in decisions. [6]

Following this initiative, more articles criticizing government policies and urging reforms were published in Ta-hsueh tsa-chih. Beginning in July, Chang Ching-hang, in coauthorship with Mr. Chang

Shao-wen, Mr. Hsu Jen-chen, and Mr. Pao Ching-tien, published
his long article, "An Analysis of Social Forces in Taiwan," which
painted a grim picture of social and economic development of Taiwan and severely condemned the ruling party and government. The
young intellectuals, it appeared, were beginning to speak more boldly. It is, however, difficult to judge if this trend would be per-

Chun-hsiang, and Sun Chen of National Taiwan University; Professors Hungdah Chiu and Lu Chun-pu of National Chengchi University;
Professor Ko Chun of the College of Chinese Culture; and Messrs.
Chang Shao-wen, Chen Shao-ting, Chang Ching-hang, Hsu Jen-chen,
and Pao Ching-tien. These men were at the time the core group
of the Ta-hsueh tsa-chih in which their statement appeared. Primarily drafted by Mr. Chang Ching-hang, the program basically
called for a rejuvenation of the ruling stratum, a prosperous economy, the rule of law, and an open society with pluralist values.[7]

Broadly speaking, the over-all view of this group of intellectuals could best be described as democratic, anti-Communistic, and
"realistic." Though in their program they did not dwell on the issue of Communism at any length, it was clear that they viewed the
takeover of the mainland by the Chinese Communist Party as a trag-
edy. And without saying it in so many words, they definitely looked
toward the Western democracies for inspiration and guidance. They
assumed explicitly that Taiwan could and should remain, de facto
if not de jure, an autonomous political entity for an indefinite period
to come. Their message was that effort should be made toward
political reforms in Taiwan so that Taiwan could present an alternative, i.e., an open and democratic society, to the Communist system in China. As they put it:

> We need not spend too much of our time and energies on
> something that we could not accomplish at the present
> time, given our resources. The realization of a unified

China is, of course, our ultimate goal and the ideal of our struggle; yet at the present time, the most important task is to do well in Taiwan. We must first succeed in doing well in Taiwan, which is a small place, before we can do well in a place three hundred-fold larger. Thus, to build Taiwan into a paradise that would attract all Chinese is what we can do at the present time and is where we should concentrate our utmost effort. We should achieve on Taiwan an open society, promote honesty in politics and efficiency in administration as well as provide fully for the people's livelihood. If we could make Taiwan a paradise, and make it appealing to Chinese people in all parts of the world, then Taiwan would naturally exercise a centripetal pull on the people in the mainland; if we do not succeed in strengthening ourselves, we could only sentimentally claim the mainland; and what is even worse, we could not even survive. . . . Fundamentally the solution to our problems is to modernize our nation. Only a healthy society can survive the stormy time. At the present stage, we must concentrate our effort on building an economy and making the people prosperous, protecting human rights, and establishing the rule of law as well as an open society with pluralist values. [8]

Specifically, the platform on rejuvenation of the ruling stratum urged incorporating the "mainstream of society" into the decision-making process and presenting the people with a "new image." In traditional China, the statement asserted, the political process and decision-making had always operated from the higher echelon downward. The decision-makers tended to make policies guided either by abstract ideology or precepts from the classics; or they made decisions based on their personal views of things. This method, however, if workable in the past, could no longer be useful at the present time. Society in Taiwan had been going through a period of rapid change, and the people were becoming fairly well educated. For an efficient government and to adapt to the realities, the ruling elite needed new blood; a brain trust composed of the best experts available was absolutely imperative, and it needed to be charged with planning for the long-range development of the nation and advise decision-makers in the making of policy. Furthermore, the government had to elicit the enthusiasm of the people by giving itself a "new image" through the adoption of a new style of doing things and a new face. New men needed to be recruited en masse into the decision-making stratum, and a "drastic change should be brought about vis-à-vis the group of the people's representatives at the national level who for the past twenty years had been supported [illegible]

[illegible] of Taiwan. Assaulting the secrecy of the military expenditure, the statement forcefully argued for reduction of the armed forces along with making part of the army into a "production corps," reducing the period of conscription to one year, and providing fully for the welfare of retired officers and soldiers.

On the issue of diplomatic expenditures, the platform encouraged friendly relations with other states but maintained that it should not be done at too high a price. International trade, it was urged, should aim at "making money" to aid the economic development of the nation and should not be sacrificed to diplomacy, in particular, for purchasing support at the United Nations. The urge to do so, the statement warned, if perceived and exploited by other nations, would not only impair the nation's interests but would make Taiwan a laughing stock in the world community.

Along the same line, the platform demanded the elimination of overlap, inefficiency, and corruption within the bureaucracy and government-operated enterprises. The statement suggested that an efficient administration and management needed to be set up, or any amount of state investment could not help but lead to greater waste of state resources.

Going beyond measures for controlling expenditure, the statement demanded giving full power to government officials in charge of finance and economy to plan and manage the economic development of Taiwan. "In modern societies, particularly a society in need of rapid development such as ours, economic collapse may lead to disintegration. . . . We only know about the development of economy, but we dare not delegate full power to government officials in the fields of finance and economy to coordinate natural resources and deal with all types of obstacles. . . . Without this kind of delegation of power the nation could not engage in the struggle of economic warfare of our times; and a nation without a sound economic base can not aspire to modernization."[10]

The platform section on the rule of law gave a brief exposition of the concept of government by law and proposed wide-ranging reforms of different components of the political structure in Taiwan. The rule of law, the statement suggested, refers to the "institutionalization" of the government and an administrative system guided by laws and supported by a sound personnel system. Laws and ordinances must be streamlined and aimed at the public interest, the statement declared.

For the administrative branch of the government, the statement emphasized protection of basic human rights and promotion of the public welfare.

What the citizens complain about most often at the present time is the lack of protection of basic human rights; at any time, personal rights and liberties can be violated due to the arbitrary use of power by government functionaries. Further, there have been so many laws and ordinances that the people feel that their freedoms are severely restricted. . . . The citizens of modern society demand of their government only, negatively, that their freedoms and rights will not be violated; they will be satisfied if the government refrains from doing anything to deprive them of their freedoms and rights. Yet in this regard, the power of the government seems to have been expanded too much. On the other hand, as to tackling problems and promoting the social welfare, the people demand an active and efficient government. Yet, in this regard, the government appears to have done too little.[11]

The reasons for this situation were seen as twofold: first, the government still held on to the traditional authoritarian ideal.

Second, due to long years of holding power without the challenge of an opposition party, the ruling elite had succumbed to the habit of using power arbitrarily. To achieve the goal of the rule of law, it was said, the government had to give up outdated ideas suitable for the simple age of the past and, facing the demands of the entrepreneur class and the intellectual community, establish the rule of law and

viduals from without and corruption of the personnel from within. For these reasons, the integrity of the judiciary can not be maintained. No doubt, the autonomy of the judiciary must bring with it some degree of curtailment of the vested interests of the ruling elite; yet they must realize that only through such a self-imposed curtailment of their interests can their long-term interests be protected. The administrative branch should not interfere with the judiciary; on the contrary, it should encourage the judiciary branch to deal severely with any high-ranking officials who have violated the laws. . . . Of late, to combat the corruption of the judiciary, the government has used the Bureau of Investigation to check the abuse of power by the judges. Yet instead of preventing the corruption of the judiciary, this method has created another type of interference with the judiciary.[12]

The solution, the statement proposed, lay in securing absolute autonomy of the judiciary branch as well as a vigorous and sound system of selecting, training, promoting, and sufficiently compensating judges so that they would be respected as a moral force within society and act accordingly. The example of England, the statement suggested, had much to teach in this regard.

The statement severely condemned the people's representatives at the national level as an aging privileged group and urged, by

implication, their replacement through reelections at regular inter-
vals.

> For more than twenty years, we have supported and
> kept intact a privileged elite group which is large,
> aging, and, broadly speaking, cut off from the masses.
> Though on the surface this policy has maintained the
> legitimacy of the government, even formally they could
> not represent those people who, some twenty-three
> years ago when the election took place, had not yet
> reached the age of twenty. This young generation, i.e.
> people age 43 or under, who account for two-thirds
> of the population [under the jurisdiction of the govern-
> ment] at the present time, did not have the opportunity
> to elect their representatives at the national level.
> Even for those age 43 and above, it could not be argued
> that once they had cast their votes the issue of repre-
> sentation was decided forever. Further, the government
> has paid a very high price in shouldering this burden; it
> not only casts a shadow on the reputation of the govern-
> ment in the international community, it has also deprived
> the people of a group of representatives who genuinely
> care and represent their interests. [13]

Turning to the censorial branch of the government, the statement argued for the utility of an opposition party as the ultimate
tool for controlling abuse of power. "For the modernization of our
nation, we could not but hope that the ruling party and government
would take the initiative in establishing a two-party system. If this
is not feasible, given the peculiar circumstances at the present time,
it would seem desirable that the ruling party divide itself into two
parts and take turns governing the nation through choice by the
people's votes. They would thus engage in competition, which would
be judged by the people, and exert their utmost in serving the
people. . . . If this reform can not be done at the present time,
we propose as a second best solution, that the Control Yuan should
be completely reformed."[14] The measures for reforms, the statement suggested, should take into account both structure and personnel problems. The power of impeachment, to be effective, the
statement said, needed to be backed up by the power of questioning
officials and approving the government budget, while members of
the Control Yuan should be selected for their sense of justice and
courage through civil service examinations.

Finally, the platform on an open society with pluralist values called for a democratic society in which the wisdom and creativity of men would be developed to the highest degree. Orthodoxy in thought, the statement asserted, was not a prerequisite for unification of the nation; on the contrary, in modern societies, diverse thoughts and views had to be tolerated so that, through creativity,

racy and freedom, but we have not seen the flowering of an open society. For the past twenty years, we have made great efforts in the development of our economy, utilizing every bit of our material resources; yet the wisdom of the heart and mind of every Chinese has hardly been developed. . . . The problem we face today is that for the past two decades, with the development of our educational system we have been influenced by Western civilization, and we appreciate not only the strong points of Western civilization, but also its weaknesses. Yet our ruling elite, fearing the weak points of Western civilization, has also rejected its strong points. Moreover, we are faced with a powerful, effective, and totalitarian enemy. Since we have been defeated by this enemy, everybody seems intent on learning from them; however, their strong points precisely are those that strangle the humanity of men. [15]

To create an open and democratic society, the statement went on to suggest, the ethical system based on harmony and mutual trust of interpersonal relationships for which the ancients had been striving for thousands of years should be restored; and the security police which destroyed the mutual trust and harmony of the innocent people had to be severely curbed. Furthermore, "the authoritarian and eight-legged educational system," both at home and at school, which emphasized instilling worship of authority, had to be replaced by education for the development of creativity and personality. Protection of academic freedom, availability of important works of Chinese scholars who, for one reason or other, had stayed on the mainland; access to the study of mainland China for all; and, last of all, the people's right to travel and study abroad were also urged. Summing up the program, the statement declared:

> Our ideal society is a just, free, democratic, fair, open, and wealthy society; a society without fears, monopoly, and violence. The dream of the people throughout the world for such a way of life is a most powerful urge; and if a government is not capable of leading its people in realizing this ideal, it should, at the very least, not interfere with the development of the trend. Any government that goes against the tide will definitely be washed out by the rising waves. As Chinese [we realize] that this ideal is what our ancients had been striving for for many thousands of years, and if we could make Taiwan into a paradise of our dream, it would become a beacon of light for the seven-hundred million Chinese [in the mainland] .[16]

This program of political reforms, as a collective work, reflected the ideas and views of many men and minds. Thus, the statement is somewhat repetitious and stylistically clumsy. Signs of give and take were evident at many points. For example, the legislature and the people's representatives at the national level were severely criticized, yet the statement fell short of calling for their replacement through a "comprehensive reelection," a position which Mr. Chen Shao-ting, one of the signatories, had already taken.[17] Likewise, the issue of an opposition party was dealt with but not vigorously pursued. Apparently fearing that too emphatic an advocacy of a two-party system might jeopardize the whole program, a compromise was reached: "complete reform of the Control Yuan" to curb the abuse of power.

Also conspicuously absent was any specific discussion of the problems of political prisoners, though Professor Lin Chen-hung of the Philosophy Department of National Taiwan University had already urged an amnesty for political prisoners in Taiwan. In the opinion of Professor Lin, political prisoners in Taiwan were of three types: extreme anti-Communist liberals who used the yardstick of Western democracy in their criticisms of government, leftists provoked by the inequality they saw around them, and native Taiwanese dissatisfied with their treatment by the mainlanders. The first category, he felt, should be treated by the government as friends; the second and third groups, given the social progress made in the past decades and the need for solidarity, should also be pardoned according to the merit of their cases.[18]

theless, the program as a whole expressed the fears and hopes of the young intellectual community and in a sense served as an agenda for the debate on political reforms in the early seventies in Taiwan. The response of the mass media, of university professors and students, and of society at large was electric and immediate. The issue of the Ta-hsueh tsa-chih in which the program appeared went into a sixth printing, which by any conventional measurement must be taken as an indication of the considerable attention it attracted.

In the months following the publication of this program, the ferment for political reforms reached a crescendo. More and more intellectuals, particularly university students, took part in an ever wider circle of agitation and activities, thus exerting a severe pressure on the party and government. There was a sense of excitement and expectation. Professors and students gave speeches, published articles, held forums, and signed proclamations. The newspapers, tightly controlled by the government as they were, joined in to a certain degree. Editorials appeared urging political reforms, though they tended to take a modest position so as not to risk confrontation with the party and government. The ruling party, partly dictated by necessity, partly to placate the public clamor, also came through with a promise of reforms. In emergency meetings of the Central Advisory Committee and the Central Committee of the Nationalist Party held two days after the expulsion of the Republic of China from the United Nations, the party leadership pledged, among other things, to review party leadership style at all levels and streamline party organization, to recruit men of talent into government service, and to strengthen the people's representative organs at the national level "in accordance with the principle of a democratic constitutional system. "[19]

Two episodes taking place at this time well illustrated the climate of public opinion toward reforms. Mr. Wang Hsing-ching, a graduate from National Taiwan University, declined a scholarship from the University of Mississippi so that, as he explained in a letter to his sponsor, he could dedicate his life to his nation in time of crisis and need.[20] He and a number of National Taiwan University students issued a statement in November 1971 pledging to share their fate with the people living in Taiwan and urging the government to rely on the people in the fight for survival. Corruption and privileges, they demanded, must be eliminated; and those who deserted Taiwan with their funds should be severely punished.[21] Immediately Mr. Wang was proclaimed a "national hero," a model for youth. If his views were highly emotional and nationalistic and his proposals for reforms simplistic, this apparently did not detract from their appeal to society at large.[22] A young Nationalist Party member, Mr. Ho Wen-cheng, in an open letter to youth, also pledged himself to campaign for public office the following year and challenged his readers to do likewise.[23]

The program for political reforms by the Ta-hsueh group, nevertheless, did not go unchallenged. In December 1971, 336 university and college professors signed a declaration urging political reforms.[24] They aimed at presenting an alternative program. Primarily drafted by Professor Chang Ya-yung of National Chengchi University, an expert on Dr. Sun Yat-sen's teachings and comparative constitutional law,[25] and signed by many professors of the Three People's Principles and deans of student affairs, the declaration asserted that "the problem facing the world today is a problem of cultural value. . . . If mankind were to successfully defeat communism, to avoid entering a new dark age, it must protect and promote traditional values and ideals, and on the basis of which create a new cultural spirit." It proposed, among other things, reform of the people's representative organs at the national level in accordance with the principle that they must represent the entire country; recruitment of men of talent into governmental service without any distinction of age, regional differences, or party affiliation, but limited to those possessed of "knowledge of the true nature of Communism"; strengthening the unity of all anti-Communist

forces in Taiwan and abroad, consolidation of the leadership core--
"in this time of trial, we all the more need the most experienced,
the most esteemed, the most wise, and the most steadfast old pilot
. . . to lead us"; elimination of corruption and privilege; improvement of the living standards of peasants, workers, and fishermen;
and tightening of control over the activities of Chinese Communist

A more harsh criticism of the reform program by the Ta-
hsueh group came from Mr. Hu Chiu-yuan, publisher of the _Chun-
ghwa Monthly_. A member of the Legislative Yuan and a well-known
intellectual with a long, colorful career in politics and academia
behind him at the age of sixty, Mr. Hu Chiu-yuan still exercised some
influence on a portion of the intellectuals both in Taiwan and abroad.
While urging political reforms, particularly curtailment of privileges
and corruption, he held fast to his ideas of self-reliance, both in
military defense and economic development, and a search for opportunities to provoke revolution on the Chinese mainland.   Relying on
the support of the United States and Japan was the ultimate folly, he
believed.   He ridiculed the thesis of "making Taiwan a paradise" as
the dream of fools; and the platform on economic development as
proposed by the _Ta-hsueh_ group appeared to him to be nothing less
than "parasitism," the defense of the wealthy few at the expense of the
many.   He rejected the argument for "complete reelection of the
people's representatives at the national level" as undercutting the
legitimacy of the government and the basis of constitutional rule and
leading inevitably to an independent Taiwan completely severed from
China.[27]   His criticisms and proposals for actions, however, given
the climate of opinion at that time, somehow failed to elicit much
response from the young intellectuals in Taiwan.

In January 1972, with Professor Yang Kuo-shu, Professor Chen
Ku-ying, and Mr. Chang Ching-hang taking the initiative, the _Ta-
hsueh_ group pushed on with the publication of _Nine Treatises on the
Issues Facing the Nation_.   The essays were designed as a supple-

ment to the program of October 1971.[28] Nineteen men signed their names to this series of essays, including twelve signatories to the reform program of October 1971, although altogether about thirty or more persons took part in the preparation of the treatises.[29] Professors Hungdah Chiu, Sun Chen, and Su Chun-hsiang, having taken a more modest view on political reforms by this time, declined to sign. The issues discussed were those of human rights, an administrative personnel system, diplomacy, economic development, agriculture and the peasantry, social welfare, educational reforms, local government, and youth problems. Originally it had been planned that an essay on governmental legitimacy would be included, bringing the total to ten treatises; but because the issue was politically explosive, the idea was abandoned at the last moment. For each of the nine treatises, a discussion group was set up; and one of the signatories or, in some cases, someone other than the signatories, was assigned the task of summing up the discussion and serving as rapporteur.

The series of treatises was essentially an elaboration of the reform program presented in October 1971, proceeding from the perspective enunciated earlier. They did make an effort to come to grips with concrete measures, however, and the treatises abounded with all types of recommendations. Yet on the whole, little new ground was broken, with the exception of the issue of social welfare for the peasantry, the workers, and the poor, which was given much more weight and delineated more clearly.

Writing as the rapporteur on the treatise on agriculture and the peasantry, Mr. Tsai Hung-chin proposed a five-point program:

Strengthen the cooperation of the Peasant Associations in the field of marketing, so that they can protect themselves against the exploitation of the middlemen.

Provide the peasants with accurate and timely information as to the selection of crops in anticipation of the needs of the markets.

Nurture genuine peasant leaders and give them encouragement and support so that they can serve the interests of the peasants.

Develop a social welfare program for the peasants, not only to aid the poor in the villages, but also to equalize the standard of living in the cities and the countryside.

Provide clinics and hospitals for the peasants, particularly in poor and isolated areas and, as soon as pos-

poverty; that economic and social development should complement each other, taking into account the issue of fair distribution of social wealth; that the entrepreneur class should be induced through tax policy to contribute to social welfare programs; and that university students and other segments of society concerned with social justice should be mobilized into a social service corps to help implement social welfare programs.[31]

Taken together, the statement of October 1971 and the Nine Treatises rounded off the program for political reforms by the young university professors and students. Of the many demands and proposals, four issues emerged as the most crucial and urgent:

1. The affirmation of democratic values, human rights, and fundamental freedoms.

2. Youth participation in politics and university affairs.

3. Recruitment of young men into governmental service and reelection of the people's representatives at the national level.

4. Social welfare for the peasants, workers and poor.

Until the early part of 1973 when the ferment began to ebb, these issues were the predominant concerns of the young intellectuals.

The goal of the intellectual ferment for political reforms was clearly an open, democratic society. However, it was also plain that political activities in Taiwan would be influenced by traditional values and styles. Realizing this, a number of university professors concentrated their efforts on clarifying and affirming democratic values as well as assaulting the dead hands of the past. Among them, Professors Hu Fu, Wen Chung-i, and Yuan Sung-hsi did the most. In particular, Professor Hu Fu of the Department of Political Science at National Taiwan University, an authority on Chinese constitutional law, was clear in his exposition and eloquent in his formulation. In March 1972, he wrote:

> . . . the purpose of our state is the realization of fundamental human rights and the rule of law. No doubt, it is for this purpose that we fight against communism. The government is the tool of the state, and any policy and measure must be directed toward this; otherwise, they are without any basis. Of course, fundamental human rights are not without any limits; yet imposing limits must be in accordance with the constitution. This is the meaning of the rule of law. From the perspective of the government, in order to maintain constitutional rule and protect human rights, it should not arbitrarily impose any limitation for temporary convenience or any other purposes. To promote economic prosperity and social progress, politics must be modernized. And political modernization must relate to democracy and freedom. . . .
>
> Suspicion and misunderstanding of democracy and freedom tend to lead to the creation of "taboos." Taboos are extralegal criteria, lacking in precise delineations, and given subject judgment, can not but make for diffused pressures. Opinions and actions may not violate the laws; but they might be prohibited by the taboos. . . .
>
> . . . With the removal of the taboos, vitality will be restored, and "formalism" will lose its protection; then everyone will be lively and genuinely engaged in the creation of new things. [32]

Again, in early 1973, he wrote:

Our value is the promotion of freedom and democracy.
Freedom and democracy are not the expression of emo-
tion; rather they are the embodiment of reason. In
other words, it is a way of life based on reason, on
the dignity and worth of the individual, and with emphasis on autonomy, equality and the rule of law.

based on the concept of democratic participation. In
any country, the number of men in power is limited;
thus, the importance of participation does not lie only
in direct participation in the political process; it also
lies in indirectly expressing one's views on political
decisions, without being suspected of any ultramotives.
. . . Participation will not only make for a stronger
self, and enhance the trust in political efficacy, it will
also help bring about a sense of responsibility and
identity. . . .[33]

Likewise, Mr. Wen Chung-i, an anthropologist and research
staff member at the Academia Sinica, emphatically argued for
change and adoption of democratic procedure. Condemning reform
by administrative fiat as relying only on "men of talent," and
being effective only in trifling matters, he opted for democracy
against traditional patterns. He wrote:

First of all, we must consider the strengthening of democratic politics. . . . Compared with any other methods
or means, democratic politics is more effective in competing with totalitarian rule. . . . The manifestations of
democracy are many: voting is one of them; so is popular participation. . . . Therefore, we must adjust and
change any policy, laws or ordinances which hinder the
development of democratic politics, so that we can meet
the needs of our situation. . . .

During the time of reform, the rationalizations most often resorted to by those against reforms are the protection of traditional culture and the stability of society.
But they are mistaken. The reformists have never desired the destruction of traditional culture, neither have
they hoped for the disruption of social stability. It is
only that they, unlike the traditionalists, do not cling to
traditions, do not think that all traditions are good and
workable in our time. The reformists selectively preserve part of the tradition, and by doing so, aim at the
betterment of social life at a higher stage. . . .

In time, the forces for reform and anti-reform might
find themselves in two opposing camps; yet they might
at the same time exist in a group. For example, a
political organization claiming reform as its goal might
still be anti-reform due to a mistake in policy-making
which turns out to be against reforms. Therefore, we
must be very careful in our decision-making, taking
special care of the interests of the majority of society,
so that we may not contradict ourselves without knowing
it. . . .[34]

Professor Yuan Sung-hsi, of the Department of Political Science at National University, also spoke along this line. What was
needed in the ultimate analysis, he said, were democracy and science, both closely related to education, through which these two
values could be implanted in the hearts and minds of the citizens.

Democracy is not only a political institution, it is also
a way of life and a value system. If we only adopt a
democratic political institution without adopting the values supporting it, the institution can not operate for
long. . . .

But, after adopting the Western democratic political institutions, how (can) we induce the people to universally
accept the values of democracy, such as the protection
of basic human rights and the change of government
through the wishes of the people? There is not, except
by means of education, particularly formal education,
any other effective means. . . .

I hold the view that at the present time, civic education
at schools, apart from emphasizing national spirit,
should also, for the long-range interest of the nation,
stress the education of a democratic spirit. . . . A
civic education which emphasizes democratic spirit is
not only concerned with the inculcation of democratic

[illegible faded text]

portable thinking. . . . Anyone trained in this kind of
vigorous thinking naturally is immune from the influence
of the evil communist totalitarian political system. . . .

If we affirm that science is a method of thinking, and if
we further affirm that science is what we need at this
time, then we must start from the basic things. We
must train our children in this type of thinking from primary school on. . . . Scientific thinking methods . . .
should also be strengthened in middle school and college. . . .[35]

In October 1972, in the wake of the establishment of diplomatic relations between Peking and Tokyo, when the Republic of China
was faced with its darkest hour, democracy and freedom were given
a resounding affirmation in a forum sponsored by the Ta-hsueh tsa-
chih. Some twenty-five intellectuals took part, including Mr. Tao
Pai-chuan, a well-known member of the Control Yuan and political
commentator, Professors Wen Chung-i, Wang Shao-po, Chou Tao-chi,
Hu Fu, Sun Chen, Yuan Sung-hsi, Wei Chen-tung, Chen Ku-ying,
and Yang Kuo-shu, and Mr. Chen Shao-ting, Mr. Chang Shao-wen,
and Mr. Po Yu-hung. In the forum the role and mission of Taiwan
in the future development of China was affirmed: a free and democratic Taiwan which would serve as a beacon of light for people on
the mainland and a building block for a free and democratic China
in the future. This goal, the participants asserted, was the raison
d'être of their life. Achievements in many fields by the Chinese

Communists were recognized, yet the Communist system as the wave of the future was emphatically rejected. 36

As a collateral to democratic values, freedom of speech and thought for university students was championed most eloquently by Professor Chen Ku-ying. In a moving passage, Professor Chen Ku-ying laid bare his feelings and urged his students to assert their rights:

> I use the title "Toleration and Understanding" for this book of collected articles [because] it expresses my concern with basic human rights and denotes the meaning of education through love and trust. . . . Some friends of mine were shocked that I had dared to take on issues relating to "security." A friend asked me if I had any special background to protect me. I came to Taiwan with my parents when I was in my teens. More than a decade ago, my parents passed away. For more than twenty years, I grew up in a very difficult set of circumstances. I have neither any special background nor any connection to protect me. If there is any support, it is my purity. . . . I grew up in Taiwan, in this "green house," I have never heard of any heretical ideas, or breathed any heretical air; neither have I participated in any organized group. I live my own life. Yet as I am an idealist, I can not help but be critical of the realities. . . . I seek reforms by peaceful means, and I have never believed that "violence" could bring progress to any society. But I emphatically believe that if political reforms do not keep pace with the progress of society, violent change can not be prevented.

> Finally, I think I have the right to say a few words to our elders: the potential of youth is an immense source of strength for the progress of our country. [If you] trust them, and let them develop their potential, it will bring renewed opportunity to the nation in crisis; if you distrust them and try to curb them, even the strongest embankment you build will crumble. I also want to say a word to our young friends: Our government is an organ for the protection of and service to the people; our officials are our servants. Let us speak our minds without fear, for freedom of speech is our natural right. 37

This clarion call had a stimulating effect on the university students, particularly since they had for years been restless under the control of the Office of the Dean of Students and been provoked by the censorship imposed on their newspapers and journals. This censorship had been criticized as lacking in any criteria, being incompetently implemented due to the personnel in charge, and insisting that only praise of the status quo was permissible.[38]

out freedom of speech; otherwise, this forum would be impossible. But, we can also definitely say that the censorship imposed on us is absolutely unreasonable; otherwise, this forum would be unnecessary."[39] Among the professors invited to speak, with the exception of Professor Chin Chu-lien, dean of the School of Engineering, who took a modest view, all of the speakers argued for the necessity of freedom of speech for the promotion of human dignity and the progress of society. Professor Su Chun-hsiang, a visiting law professor trained in West Germany, approached the issue from the perspective of constitutional law and dwelt upon the necessity of freedom of speech as an instrument for the development of personality and human dignity. He urged that the university train free and responsible men.[40] Professor Yang Kuo-shu spoke of the diverse degrees of the need for freedom, given different individual psychological make-ups. He argued that not only was freedom of speech limited by laws and self-discipline but more importantly, its exercise would promote a system of checks and balances among diverse opinions in a market of ideas. As he saw it, intellectuals particularly needed freedom of speech so that they could criticize defects in politics and contribute effectively to reform. He proposed that, for the guidance of student publications, a joint committee composed of administrators, faculty, and students be set up to deal with any problems, with emphasis placed on reaching a compromise through consensus.[41]

This theme of the need for freedom of speech was echoed both by Professor Wang Shao-po and Professor Wang Wen-hsing. Professor Wang Shao-po in particular stressed moral courage, saying that "only those who have the moral courage to accept the consequences of their actions have the right to freedom of speech."[42] Professor Chen Ku-ying spoke at length in a speech frequently interrupted by enthusiastic applause. He first asserted the importance of freedom of speech, both for individuals and society. Citing the great height of cultural achievement in the Spring and Autumn and Warring States periods, he deplored the fact that in contemporary times, people enjoyed less freedom of speech than in ancient times. Both men in power and intellectuals had deserted the cause, he said, the former for fear that the exercise of freedom of speech would severely affect their positions of power, the latter for fear that any criticism would be labeled harmful to "national security." He hailed young students as idealists, enthusiastic and infused with a sense of justice. They were, he said, the driving force of social reforms and progress. To unleash the potentials of youth, he proposed that there be set up on the university campus a "democratic wall" or "freedom wall" or, if the designation was too politically sensitive, a "Voice of Taita Wall" in which the university community would be encouraged to express their opinions on any matters through the use of posters.[43]

Dean of Students Chang Teh-pu, a military man before assuming his new post at the university, rather ably defended the position of the university authorities. Conceding that freedom of speech was guaranteed by the constitution, he emphasized that responsibility went along with its exercise. He was, however, more concerned with refuting the charge against censorship and its incompetent implementation. Referring to several cases, he argued that review of student publications by university authorities should be seen in the light of a desire to protect students against possible violation of laws.[44] Nevertheless, when the time came for the students to speak, it was plain that he had not convinced them. Also citing facts and figures, the students, including Mr. Wang Hu-su, newly elected president of the Student Association, Mr. Hung Shen-hsiang, president of Fa Yen, the student publication of Law College students, Mr. Lin Shao-pin, editor-in-chief of Taita Ching-lien, and Mr. Lin Chun-wen of the Ta-hsueh hsin-wen [University news] without exception condemned the censorship and stated they would not be satisfied with anything less than its abolition.[45] Moreover Mr. Wang Hu-su demanded that the Garrison Command be more circumspect in dealing with university students, that if there were no sufficient grounds to justify it, students not be arbitrarily summoned for interviews. This practice, he said, led to unnecessary fear and psychological pressure on the students.[46]

Beyond protection of human rights and freedoms, the university professors and students also demanded youth participation in politics and university affairs. After much agitation and deliberation, the

[illegible faded text]

kind of evaluation of the faculty, and to participate more in politics, either helping candidates in their campaigns or directly seeking public office. Professor Chen Ku-ying was again his eloquent self, attacking denial of freedom of speech by the security police, deploring lack of opportunity for youth participation, and condemning emphasis on orthodoxy in thought. These three factors, as he saw it, inevitably led to political alienation. Returning to his favorite theme, he forcefully called for a student movement. "Student movement," he said, "is the highest expression of a sense of justice and responsibility; it is a selfless act induced not by material interests, but by conscience. . . . We need not fear student movement. If student movement is risky, it is not because the students are dangerous; rather it is because the society is faced with crisis. Only a student movement, a self-awakening movement, a patriotic movement, could lead to social progress and defend the nation in crisis."[48] To push the student movement, he proposed that the university build an "academic activity center" equipped with large lecture halls and seminar rooms for the use of faculty and students. Before the building was completed, the Office of the Dean of Students should designate the sporting fields as the "democratic forum" and permit students to freely express their views and give speeches at the flag platform.[49] This proposal, as could be anticipated, was received by the young students with a great deal of enthusiasm.

Three weeks later, through the initiative of Mr. Wang Hsing-ching and Mr. Wang Hu-su, twenty-three student leaders from National Taiwan University, National Chengchi University, and National Normal University issued a declaration calling for student action. They proposed a six-point program: to work for awakening and self-strengthening of youth; to urge popular participation in politics; to urge strengthening of government administrative function; to eliminate the "traitors" who have deprived the people of their opinions; to remove obstacles to social progress; and to maintain the independence and integrity of sovereignty.[50] For the implementation of this declaration, student leaders of National Taiwan University met on December 8, 1971, with Professors Yang Kuo-shu and Wu Chung-hsien serving as advisors. They concluded that university students should be mobilized to go into society, to serve as spokesmen of the poor and as a bridge between government and the people.[51] It was decided that a "social service army" should be organized. However, due to the sensitivity of the term "army," it was later changed to "social service team," and then to "social service corps." In a sense, the term "social service corps" was not an accurate appellation, for the emphasis was placed on investigation rather than on service. Five areas were designated as subject matters for investigation: rural problems, the poor in the cities, relations between police and citizens, labor problems, and local elections.

The administration of the university, after some hesitation, agreed to support the project. It allocated some NT$100,000 for expenses, and through its connections, arranged for the cooperation of different governmental organs. At the beginning of January 1972, the project was put into effect. A campaign for recruitment of volunteers was initiated on the campus; within a few days, 150 students were chosen through a screening process which gave priority to language ability, in particular the ability to speak Taiwanese, and to the compatibility of academic training and the subject matter of investigations. The corps was divided into seventeen groups. After two days of orientation, they were dispatched to all corners of the island, visiting no less than seventy-two townships and villages in sixteen counties and cities. Altogether the students spent ten days conducting their field work. The project was completed on January 22.

Apparently the project caught the imagination of the student body, and the reactions of society at large were mostly favorable. Newspaper comments emphasized on the whole the significance of student participation. However, the project also suffered from a

number of defects. To begin with, though the project had been supported by university authorities, there was lingering doubt as to the
desirability of such large-scale student participation.   Furthermore,
preparation left quite a bit to be desired: the period of orientation
was too short, the questionnaires tended to be irrelevant, and the
qualifications of the volunteers did not prove equal to the tasks.   In

vestigation were not made public.   As a result, students and the
university administration blamed each other.   While the students
may have tended towards muckraking, the university administration
and the government presumably had an interest in seeing that the
reports were not too critical.   To a large extent, political factors
apparently accounted for the stillbirth of the final reports.   Nevertheless, even if the project did not accomplish much, it dramatized
concern for the poor and afforded students an opportunity to have a
close look into the darker side of society.

In agitating for political structural reforms, the young intellectuals soon focused on the problems of recruiting young men of
talent into governmental service and rejuvenating the people's representative organs at the national level.   The debates were heated
and the recommendations numerous.   The Nationalist Party leadership, in promising to recruit men of talent into governmental service, was thinking in traditional terms: political restoration needs
moral, loyal, and competent men.   The implication was that excep-
tional men should be recruited and promoted without regard for the
operation of the personnel system.   The appointment of Chiang
Ching-kuo to the position of premier was justified on these grounds.[52]
The young intellectuals had their own views.   The program of political reform presented in the Ta-hsueh tsa-chih in October 1971
pleaded for incorporation of new blood into the decision-making process and for creation of a brain trust of younger men with expert
knowledge.   Without saying it in so many words, it came close to
urging a technocracy on the government.   As elaborated by Chang

Ching-hang and Hsu Jen-chen later, a brain trust was needed to aid policy-making at the highest echelon of government and for the institutionalization of the civil service. Forcefully, if somewhat dogmatically, they argued that men of "first-rate talent" must come from specific academic institutions: in the United States, they come from Harvard; in England, from Oxford and Cambridge; in Japan, from Tokyo University; and by the same analogy, in Taiwan, they must come from the leading universities. As for implementation of policy, they urged that the civil service be institutionalized: the right men in the right position and promotions by merit and merit alone. [53]

Along a somewhat different line, Professor Hu Fu argued that the crucial characteristic needed in men was a spirit of achievement and commitment to change. The policy-making echelon, he said, should be men of principle, of broad views and sound judgement, compassionate towards others and yet self-disciplined. In a word, he argued, they should be statesmen, and their training ground properly should be that of party politics. He urged the ruling party to recruit and nurture men with such qualities and prepare them for policy-making positions. Those clever in speech and insinuating in countenance, he warned, could never be trusted with the task of political reforms. The experts he saw as executors of policy; knowledge and honesty were required of them. Knowledge, he suggested, could be acquired through education and training; honesty, through the influence of society norms and individual experience. [54] Citing the experiences of the United States, Mr. Lin Pu-pai recommended that men of talent not employed by the government be invited to testify on diverse matters to supplement the use of talented men in administrative positions. [55]

Amidst the discussion and debate, a few unconventional ideas emerged. Mr. Yin Tsou took to task the concept of "men of talent," arguing that they were no more than nuts and bolts in a complicated machine, the creation of which must take planning, training, and experimentation. To seek men of talent ready-made, he concluded, was to put the cart before the horse. Crucial in his view was knowing what type of trained manpower was needed and proceeding accordingly to produce them. [56] This writer, assuming the role of devil's advocate, also addressed himself to the issue. He argued that for the development of democracy, which demands that society exercise control of government, it might not be desirable for all men of talent to be recruited by government. "Take communication and mass media, for example. All governments, without exception, are engaged in propaganda; and the manpower and resources at their disposal are far greater than the privately-owned mass media. Under such circumstances, if all the experts in communication were recruited by the government, the capacity of the government in propa-

at the national level was first brought into the open by Professor Chow Tao-chi of the College of Chinese Culture. Before the supplementary election to the people's representative organs in 1969, he had cautiously proposed adoption of three measures: that those people's representatives at the national level who were old, physically weak, and unable to perform their functions retire; that those who had violated the laws be duly prosecuted and required to give up their positions; and that younger men of special talents and achievements be recruited to participate in the work of the people's representative organs without assuming the power and responsibility of the people's representatives.[58]

Two years later, "more than ever convinced of the seriousness of the problem, [he] became more bold, and after long considerations, decided to take risks."[59] Professor Chow Tao-chi proposed four methods for the solution of the problems, which later were expanded to six. They were:

1. The members of the provincial Assembly and the Assembly of the City of Taipei shall concurrently serve as members of the National Assembly, and the enlarged National Assembly shall then elect a certain number of new members to the Legislative Yuan and the Control Yuan. They shall all serve as members of the first parliament (with life tenure). Two rules shall guide the use of this method. First, when the original National Assembly has less than four hundred

members, the President shall appoint additional members according to the principle of "universality." Second, for the election of new members to the Legislative Yuan and the Control Yuan, the President shall nominate candidates from the rosters of legal political parties and social organizations in accordance with the principles of "selectivity" and "universality."

2. The National Assembly, the Legislative Yuan and the Control Yuan shall separately or jointly elect additional members to the three people's representative organs. They shall all serve as members of the first parliament (with life tenure). Two rules shall govern the use of this method. First, the President shall nominate candidates to the three bodies according to the principle of "selectivity" and "universality" from the roster of men of talent. Second, the three bodies shall either separately or jointly elect their new members.

3. By the combination of popular election and Presidential appointment, the new members shall serve as the members of the second parliament with definite terms.

4. By the combination of popular election and Presidential appointment, the new members shall serve as the members of the first parliament with life tenure. Two rules shall govern the use of the third and fourth methods: First, those original members of the National Assembly, the Legislative Yuan and the Control Yuan, who are physically weak and unable to perform their functions shall be persuaded to retire, effective upon the approval of the President; after their retirement, they shall continue to draw their original pay and other fringe benefits. Second, the election shall be implemented according to the constitutional law: i.e., in those areas under the jurisdiction of the government, the new members of the National Assembly and the Legislative Yuan shall be elected by the popular vote; while the members of the Control Yuan shall be elected by the Provincial Assembly of Taiwan, the Assembly of the City of Taipei, and the professional organizations. In those areas not under government control, the President shall make appointments according to the principle of "equal proportion."

5. The National Assembly, the Legislative Yuan and the Control
   Yuan shall separately elect their new members. With the
   new election, the first parliament shall come to an end.

6. The National Assembly, the Legislative Yuan, the Control
   Yuan, the Provincial Assembly of Taiwan and the Assembly

   those who have been reelected or hold government positions,
   shall continue to draw pay and other benefits according to
   special laws. [60]

The proposals of Professor Chow Tao-chi, thoughtful as they
were, were immediately challenged by Mr. Chen Shao-ting. Rapidly
emerging as the most effective spokesman of the young intellectuals
on this sensitive issue, he opted for complete reelection of the
people's representative organs.

> To achieve the goal of comprehensive political reforms, a
> most basic and absolutely necessary condition is that the
> people's representatives at the national level must be re-
> elected. . . . To be sure, we also urge improving admin-
> istrative efficiency . . . yet this is not equivalent to polit-
> ical reforms. The political reforms we demand must refer
> both to political reforms as well as political innovation,
> including the restructuring of power structure and innova-
> tion in political institutions. . . . Our people's represen-
> tatives at the national level are our parliament members.
> In a democratic state the parliament is the highest organ
> of the will of the people and a cornerstone of the political
> power. In many aspects, it is the driving force of politi-
> cal progress. Therefore, when we demand political re-
> forms now, we must solve the problem of the people's rep-
> resentatives at the national level. [61]

Three reasons were adduced:

1.   That the people's representatives at the national level no
     longer represented the will of the people. "Of the more
     than two thousand people's representatives, all were elected
     in 1947, with the exception of the twenty-seven elected in
     Taiwan in 1969. . . . As they were elected some twenty-
     three years ago, how could they still represent the will of
     the people today? When they were elected to their precious
     positions, many of the soldiers who are the defenders of
     our national soil today had not yet been born; neither had
     many of the students in the universities and colleges, nor
     some of the university and college graduates. Even the
     backbone of our society today, those in their thirties and
     forties, in their prime of life, had not had the opportunity
     to cast their sacred votes. . . ."

2.   Many of the people's representatives were old and physically
     weak, and they could not perform their duties. . . . Further-
     more, as there had not been any reelection, they had become
     a privileged class, enjoying fame and emoluments; they had
     become the people's representatives with a life tenure. . . .

3.   The newly emerging social forces must be incorporated into
     the power structure. "During the past two decades, we
     sought economic and social progress in political stability.
     At the present time, the ossification of the political struc-
     ture has become, in turn, an obstacle to economic and
     social progress. To modernize the nation, to seek stabili-
     ty in progress, we must reform our power structure. . . .
     Thus, the problem of circulation of the people's represen-
     tatives has become the first priority in the search for polit-
     ical reforms. . . ."[62]

Mr. Chen Shao-ting also charged that Professor Chow Tao-chi had
not grasped the principle of constitutional democracy and that he was
far too conciliatory toward the vested interests of the people's representatives. To give the right to elect the people's representatives
to members of the National Assembly, Legislative Yuan, and Control
Yuan, he argued, violated the rights of the people; he condemned the
endorsement of both presidential appointment and popular election as
retrogressive; and to designate a category of men as "men of talent,"

he felt, smacked of elitism. The basic principle of democracy, he
declared, was equality, and any person with the qualifications for
candidacy must be given the right to compete for public office. If
"men of talent" were elected it was fine, he said, but the democratic process could not presume to know before election a category
of men designated as "men of talent"; on the contrary, any persons

walk. However, the affair turned out to be

that had not been seen in more than twenty years."[64] More than
three thousand people came to hear the debate, which went on for
two and one-half hours. The audience interrupted again and again
with applause to indicate their opinions. The China Television Company dispatched its crew to film the debate; many newspapers also
covered it. However, with the exception of the Ta-chung jih-pao,
neither the television network nor the newspapers reported on the
debate the next day. An evening newspaper published an article
by "a brilliant political scientist," apparently referring to Professor
Chow Tao-chi, but when references were made to Mr. Chen Shao-
ting, they were distorted beyond recognition.[65]

Essentially both Professor Chow Tao-chi and Mr. Chen Shao-
ting reiterated their positions during the debate. Professor Chow
Tao-chi took pains to explain that his proposals were "evolutionary,"
taking into account the factors of time, place, and men involved,
and that they aimed at something practical and workable. He
taunted Mr. Chen Shao-ting as far too idealistic and impractical,
possibly making the cure worse than the disease. Referring to his
diverse recommendations, he elaborated on a number of ambiguous
points, stressing that two of his proposed methods came close to
accomplishing complete reelection, i.e., that when new members
to the three organs of the people's representatives were elected,
the tenure of the original members automatically came to an end.[66]
He suggested that he had another formula for the solution of the
problem; yet he declined to say what it was when Mr. Chen Shao-

ting repeatedly challenged him to reveal it, to the enthusiastic applause of the audience. Mr. Chen Shao-ting adhered to his view that only a complete reelection would meet the needs of the times. The basic problem, he argued, was not men but institutions, the only obstacle being the vested interests of the members of the existing three bodies. If any political reforms were to be successful, he declared, the vested interests must be sacrificed for the greater good.[67]

Immediately following this debate, Mr. Chen Shao-ting returned to argue his case. He vigorously defended himself against detractors. He condemned as nonsense the argument that a complete reelection of the people's representatives would undermine the legitimacy and stability of the government. "Legitimacy is nothing but the will of the people, for the will of the people is the source of legitimacy. Our proposal of complete reelection aims precisely at strengthening the right of the people, in expressing the will of the people and in maintaining the legitimacy of the government."[68] Nor would he agree with the opinion that a complete reelection would undermine the stability of the government. As he viewed it, it was precisely due to the crisis that a more effective government was needed; but a more effective government could only be possible if, through reelection of the people's representatives, the basis of government were broadened and people and government worked closely together. To achieve the goal of complete reelection, he urged that one of two procedures be adopted. Either the National Assembly, acting from a sense of conscience and keeping in mind the future of the state and nation, should revise the Temporary Articles of the Constitution and provide for reelection of new representatives of the people, both in areas under government control and in Chinese communities overseas; or, if the National Assembly declined to hold a reelection, given their vested interest, the Conference of the Grand Justices should exercise its power of interpretation of the Constitution, declare the end of the first parliament, and empower the President to issue ordinances providing for reelection in both areas under government control and Chinese communities overseas.[69]

Mr. Chen Shao-ting's position, no doubt, was endorsed by the young intellectuals. The demand for complete reelection of the people's representatives was echoed again and again by university students. Many student leaders, including Mr. Wang Hu-su, Mr.

Cheng Tai-en, the editor-in-chief of the Tai-ta chien-lien, Mr. Hsu Chih-jen, the editor-in-chief of Fa Yen, and Mr. Hung Shan-hsiang, publicly demanded complete reelection.[70] In a survey conducted at National Chengchi University on December 8, 1971, only nine students among 163 approved "a substantial supplementary election" as a solution to the problem, accounting for 0.05 percent of the survey population; the overwhelming majority held the view that only a com-

hearts of the intellectuals became dominated more and more forcefully by the issue of social welfare for the peasants and workers. Since the late 1960s, reports on the plight of the peasants had been appearing in the newspapers; but it was not until the publication of An Analysis of the Social Forces in Taiwan that the problem of social justice was sharply posed. Rarely in literature from Taiwan had there been such a graphic description of the plight of the peasants and workers and of the social injustices perpetrated against them. The picture drawn was grim indeed.[73] The villages were "bankrupt." The peasants were no longer interested in tilling their land. They worked the land carelessly or simply left it uncultivated, for they could not make ends meet. The net profit from working one chia of wet rice land a year was no more than NT$4,000. Divided by a family of six, this came to less than seventy dollars per laborer per month. Thus, the monthly income of a six-member peasant household compared unfavorably with the weekly earnings of a worker in the city. Given these circumstances, the influx from countryside to city was difficult if not impossible to curb, leading to drainage of the labor force in rural areas and further decay of agricultural sectors. In the view of these authors, the decay of the agricultural sector was not an economic problem per se but a social problem of the most serious consequences.

The landlord class, the backbone of traditional society and a crucial pillar for stability, the authors of the treatise asserted, had disintegrated. This class could not compete successfully either in politics or in business, for their education was as outmoded as their resources were inadequate; furthermore, they tended to be apathetic and indifferent to society. The younger generation, driven to the cities to seek opportunity, were described as facing many frustrations and setbacks. Even the more fortunate young men who had made it into the professional class through effort and sheer determination, soon discovered that without special connections they were at a disadvantage in competition with children of the privileged class. Feeling deeply for the sufferings of their parents and relatives, they spoke on their behalf and demanded reforms; any reform measures adopted by the government would have their support.

Those not so fortunate, the study went on to suggest, could only make a living in the cities as unskilled laborers, peddlers, or bodyguards in bars and prostitution houses. In a word, they were the unemployed or semi-employed. Although not asking much when they first arrived in the cities, they very soon sensed the gross discrepancy in wealth and social injustice to which they were subjected. Bitterness and resentment turned them into mobs. In election times, they were the human sinew of demagogues and a source of disturbance and danger to society.

The situation of the workers was presented as being equally desperate. Unemployment was high; and, given population pressures, it could be expected to go higher for a decade or so. Those employed were exploited by capitalists without any protection from either government or labor unions. The exploitation of women and child labor was particularly cruel and inhuman. The easy prey of capitalists, they faced primitive working conditions and low pay. Working day and night in intolerable conditions which were both unhealthy and hazardous, they drew an average of NT$400-1,500 per month, hardly enough to live on. Male workers did not fare much better. On the average they were paid NT$1,800-2,000, hardly enough to support a family of four. As described by the authors in a moving passage:

> Their daily livings have no protection, nor do their lives
> have security. They desperately need higher wages, and
> occasionally they ask help from the labor unions. But
> when they find out that the leaders of their unions are
> none other than their employers, they can only wish that
> some day their employers might feel the pangs of con-
> science in the quiet of the night and grant them the favor.
> From time to time some of the more daring workers

might attempt to seek higher wages through bargaining
with their employers, but they usually are easily disposed of by severe political means. The other workers can only helplessly drive their wives and daughters
to seek jobs so that they can maintain a subsistence
living. Most of them live in the outskirts of the cities

[several lines illegible/faded]

even more pitiful, the study observed. Social security programs
did not help much; when accidents and disasters happened, compen-
sations were no more than NT$40,000-50,000 and no job retraining
was provided. Thus, workers were often condemned to living lives
of poverty and uselessness. Mining workers, in particular, were
threatened by accidental death. "With death, the workers' families
were left to shift for themselves, after having received the 'concern'
of the government, the 'compensation' and 'condolence' of the employers, and the 'photo-taking' of the newspaper men. It was as
if the government and the society had done their share. Yet for
the families of the deceased workers, looking at the torturous path
before them, their future was like an endless night in a dark tun-
nel. "[75]

The authors compared exploitation of workers in Taiwan with
that of nineteenth-century European workers as described in Das
Capital by Karl Marx. As they saw it, the government, due to its
experience of failure with the labor movement on the mainland, had
been afraid of labor unions and strikes, thinking that autonomous
labor unions posed a threat to the security of the state. On the
contrary, they argued, an unorganized and suppressed working labor force could easily turn into a mob. "The only force that could
tame the furious animal and turn it into a constructive force would
be that of the labor unions. Only the autonomous labor unions not
controlled by the government or the capitalists could effectively promote the interests of the workers; and only such effective labor
unions could control the potentially exploitive force. . . . When the
workers join the labor unions, they very soon become the middle

class of the industrial society, and when their needs are satisfied through the labor unions, they naturally become the supporters of the government and a force for stability. "[76]

This portraiture of peasants and workers immediately provoked a debate among the intellectuals. Professor Chen Ku-ying was deeply moved, commending the authors for their incisive analysis as well as their moral courage. [77] Professor Wang Shao-po, however, did not think the analysis was penetrating enough, referring to it rather condescendingly as "a piece of work created in an air-conditioned room. "[78]

In a forum sponsored by the Ta-hsueh tsa-chih to discuss the work, many well-known economists and government planners also took the authors to task. The authors were criticized primarily on two grounds. First, the methodology used was not scientific but rather impressionistic. Second, the tone of the analysis tended to be highly emotional; in many places judgements had been substituted for analysis. As a result, realities were distorted, giving readers an impression of impending social collapse. For example, Mr. Li Teng-hui, an agricultural expert on the staff of the Joint Commission on Rural Reconstruction, challenged the thesis that "deterioration of the countryside created the social problem." As he saw it, Taiwan was faced with "problems in the agricultural sector created by economic development." He argued that the countryside was not in decay but rather was going through a period of change; the absolute income of peasant households had not declined, but compared with other lines of employment was relatively low; and the landlord class of the past had been replaced by a new class of land owners thus creating a problem of continuity in leadership which hindered development of the rural areas. [79] Professor Wang Chou-yung of the Department of Economy at National Taiwan University dwelt upon progress and sacrifice, arguing that the decline of the landlord class was inevitable, given rapid economic changes, and so was the influx of young peasants into the cities. Explaining that he did not condone exploitation of workers by the capitalists, he nevertheless suggested that for the accumulation of capital, some degree of exploitation could not be avoided. Only after a period of time, when the consciousness of the workers had been raised, would they demand more of their share, he said; and only at that point would the government, if it were a responsible government, squeeze the fat capitalists, taking from them a part of their profit for the social welfare of the workers. [80]

Echoing Professor Wang Chou-yung, Professor Sun Chen also deplored the emotional tone of the work, stressing that progress would take time and that the intellectuals should, in urging government reforms, have more sympathy and understanding for the slowness of the process. If the majority of people preferred a slower growth rate in favor of more equitable distribution of social wealth,

and that, in a changing society with increasingly large educated masses, social injustice and exploitation could not be tolerated. On grounds of humanitarianism as well as expediency, they felt, the ruling elite must face the facts of life with courage and determination; otherwise, the stability of society would be threatened.

It is ironic that the criticisms came precisely from the expert group, the technocrats on whom the authors, particularly Mr. Chang Ching-hang, had placed so much of their hope for the survival and prosperity of society in time of crisis.

This rebuttal by the expert group, however, did not settle the issue. Letters and articles began to appear in the Ta-hsueh tsa-chih from workers and educated youth from rural areas supporting the grim description and prophecy of the authors. Mr. Chien Chien-chin, a technician and clerk in a privately owned shop, wrote of his experiences with the exploitation of laborers by capitalists, urging that only genuine and autonomous labor unions could protect their interests. [83] Mr. Wang Wen-yung, a lumber worker, wrote movingly about how he and his co-workers, all with only primary education, struggling as best they could to read the articles, had discovered for the first time in years that society genuinely cared about them and spoke on their behalf. [84] Mr. Huang Shan-lin, a college graduate from the rural district in the southern part of Taiwan, wrote of the draining of labor from the villages; the exploitation by middlemen; and the corruption and inefficiency of the Peasant Associations, the Irrigation Associations, and purchasing agents

from the Tobacco and Wine Monopoly Bureau. He supported the
thesis that the agricultural sector was faced with bankruptcy and
that this was a most serious social problem. He attacked Professor Wang Chou-yung and others, urging them to "leave the ivory
tower" and face the facts of life.[85]   Mr. Chu Ping-ching from Ping-
tung Hsien also endorsed the view of Mr. Huang Sang-lin and urged
the government to seriously tackle the problems in rural areas.[86]
Mr. Feng Yu-ping, also from Tainan, forcefully argued that decay
in the agricultural sector was not inevitable in the process of economic development but rather was the result of man-made disasters:
corruption and incompetency of government officials, monopoly of
the political process in the villages by local representatives, corruption of the agricultural associations such as Peasant Associations
and Irrigation Associations, and the traditional customs of rural
areas. These defects, he argued, could be corrected by a change
in policy without which deterioration of the agricultural sector was
inescapable.[87]

While the controversy went on, a number of industrial accidents which took place at the end of 1972 gave further impetus to
the concern with social justice. After a mine disaster just at that
time in which many miners lost their lives, Professors Chang Sih-
kuo (a visiting professor at Chiao-tung University), Chen Ku-ying,
and Wang Shao-po interviewed the families of the deceased workers.
Their description of the pitifulness of the workers' families was as
vivid as their criticisms of the government were severe.[88]   They
urged a campaign for the collection of a relief fund, which was endorsed by the Ta-hsueh tsa-chih; and money began to pour in from
the intellectual communities in both Taiwan and the United States.[89]
At the same time, the exposure of a series of unexplainable dis-
eases and the death of a number of women workers at Philco, an
American-controlled electronic company, provoked a widespread
sense of rage against the greed of capitalists and the incompetency
of the government in protecting workers against foreign capital.[90]
Professors Wang Shao-po, Hu Fu, Chang Sih-kuo, Yang Kuo-shu,
Chen Ku-ying, and others again took the government to task and
pleaded on behalf of the workers. They demanded that the government, as soon as possible, enact a Labor Law, the deliberation of
which had been going on for the past fourteen years; that the labor
insurance program be strengthened; that inspection of factory security measures be enforced; that aid be given to help organize the
workers into labor unions; and finally that care and compensation
be provided for the families of disabled and deceased workers.[91]

The ferment for political reforms, to recapitulate, had as its
goal an open and democratic society on Taiwan. For the first time
in two decades, the young intellectuals in Taiwan presented a fairly
well-thought-out program, urging wide-ranging and basic political
reforms. Many of the demands spoke to the needs of the nation
and society; and the discussions were on the whole of a high level
and sensible. The university professors and students were primarily

III. ENCOUNTER BETWEEN THE INTELLECTUALS
AND THE POWER ELITE

The relationship between the young intellectuals and the ruling elite was as ambiguous as it was complicated. In the aftermath of

his associates, in violation of their constitutional rights and despite protest from many well-known American university professors, made it clear that the use of force was not automatically ruled out.

In 1971 and 1972, university professors and students were treated to a more subtle approach by the ruling elite. But before long, tensions between the party authorities and the young intellectuals began to mount, culminating in selective persecutions of university professors and students. For their commitment to political change, many participants in the ferment for political reforms were made to pay a high price.

It is difficult to know precisely how many young men and women participated in the political ferment; yet an approximate estimate could be ascertained from diverse accounts cited earlier. If all persons taking part in activities, such as attending demonstrations and meetings, signing declarations, making speeches, and writing articles were accounted for, the number would add up to many thousands, excluding participants in Chinese communities overseas. If only those who played an activist role, such as taking the initiative in organizing demonstrations and strikes, sponsoring meetings and forums, drafting declarations, making speeches, and writing articles were counted, the total would be in the hundreds. Of these, 30 to 40 university professors, 30 to 40 students, and 20 some college graduates working in government and the business community constituted the leadership core, exercising an influence not in proportion to their number.

In age, the participants ranged from their early twenties to mid-forties, with the leadership core in their late thirties and early forties. As could be anticipated, they were predominantly males, though quite a few female students played an active role. Those in their twenties were mostly born and brought up in Taiwan, with the exception of the returned overseas Chinese student groups. Those in their thirties and forties were about equally divided between those born in mainland China and those born in Taiwan.

Given their difference in age and experience, the university students tended to take a "pure" view of politics; that is, they were more inclined to demand democracy and freedom similar to the kind they had learned about in books without giving much weight to political realities. They tended to be highly idealistic and impatient for changes. The Fa Yen Journal, for example, was dedicated to promoting democracy, freedom, human rights, and justice; it took as its motto: "Democracy and science is the only path towards rejuvenation of the nation, and freedom of speech is the necessary means of progress."[1]

On the other hand, university professors, men in government, and the business community were more inclined to take a "realist" position, seeking to accomplish the possible. Painfully aware of the influence of tradition as well as prevailing circumstances, they aimed at a program of political reforms that the ruling elite could be persuaded to accept. This, however, did not mean that they all agreed on the analysis and proposed solutions in every detail; on the contrary, differences in emphasis could be easily seen. Some demanded with vigor freedom of speech and academic freedom; others urged equal political participation, recruitment of new blood into government service, and complete reelection of the people's representatives at the national level; still others spoke passionately on behalf of the poor, taking social reforms as the first priority. Moreover, they did not reach a consensus as to their assessment of Chiang Ching-kuo's commitment to basic political changes. Many university professors had high hopes for the Premier, though quite a few were definitely skeptical. Nevertheless, they were committed to the reform program presented to the public in October 1971 and January 1972 in the Ta-hsueh tsa-chih.

Through the span of the two years, 1971-1973, the centers of protest and ferment were clearly National Taiwan University and the Ta-hsueh tsa-chih. National Taiwan University was no doubt the most prestigious university in Taiwan. It had a long tradition of freedom of inquiry; compared with other universities and colleges, it enjoyed a greater degree of autonomy from interference by the Nationalist Party and government. Many of its faculties were trained in the West where they had been exposed to Western ideas,

facing society, and beyond that, implicitly, to serve as a bridge between native Taiwanese intellectuals and their counterparts from mainland China, in anticipation that they would need to work closely together for effecting changes. For its first three years, the journal devoted a great deal of space to Western art, literature, and philosophy. Problems of modernization and the role and responsibility of intellectuals in their society were also emphasized. The expositions, however, tended to be theoretical; rarely did they deal in any systematic fashion with the problems facing Taiwan. As for a program of political reforms, there was hardly any sign of it.

In 1969 and 1970, a different group of university professors and students, primarily mainlanders, also seriously thought of publishing a journal to urge political reforms. They intended to join Chinese intellectuals in Hong Kong and the United States in a sort of communication network and cooperative effort. Many members of this group, such as Professors Yang Kuo-shu, Chen Ku-ying, and Wang Shao-po, were either members of, or closely related to Ssu-yu yen tsa-chih; however, they tended to think that the journal had turned "conservative" and had not accomplished what it set out to do. A new journal, in their view, was desperately needed. They also decided that they needed the acquiescence, if not the support, of the party if they were to succeed.

In March-April 1970, Professor Chen Ku-ying, primarily through his connection with a party functionary at National Taiwan University, succeeded in approaching Secretary General Chang Pao-shu of the Nationalist Party. He submitted a list of names of young intellectuals, and a meeting was arranged for them to meet with Mr. Chang Pao-shu and other party functionaries. The conversation was said to have been frank and pointed, with the university professors and students severely criticizing the oppression of intellectuals and the party's neglect of the social welfare of peasants and workers. Reportedly this encounter made a deep impression on party leaders, prompting Mr. Chang Pao-shu and other high-ranking party officials to make inspection tours of Taipei City and remote villages to seek opinions of the masses.[3] But as for the publication of a new journal, while party leaders at first appeared sympathetic and even committed themselves to support it financially, after prolonged discussion, nothing came of the idea and it was shelved.[4]

At the end of 1970, when the Protect Tiao-yu-tai Movement had already begun in the United States and the intellectual community in Taiwan had begun to feel its impact, the two groups of intellectuals referred to above, through a number of meetings and discussions, decided to join forces. A third group, composed primarily of professors at National Chengchi University, was also brought in. This group, including Professors Hungdah Chiu, Shih Chi-yung, and Li Chung-hui, was apparently closer to the ruling party. When they joined the Ta-hsueh tsa-chih, Professor Hungdah Chiu was a visiting professor at National Chengchi University. Professor Shih Chi-yung, a native Taiwanese, graduate of National Chengchi University, and doctor of jurisprudence from Munich University, was then deputy chief of the Fifth Section of the Secretariat General of the ruling party. His wife, Professor Li Ching-hui, also a native Taiwanese, was a graduate of National Taiwan University and the University of Paris. Both Professor Shih and Professor Li were subsequently given high posts in the party and government.

With these three groups of intellectuals coming together, a fairly elaborate reorganization of the Ta-hsueh tsa-chih took place which gave it more influence and a wider appeal. In 1971, fifty-five men and women in Taiwan and seven in the United States were listed as members of the board. Mr. Chen Shao-ting was given the post of chairman of the board; and a new position, the honorable chairman of the board, was created for Professor Hungdah Chiu. The Standing Committee of the Board listed eleven members, including Professor Hungdah Chiu, Mr. Chen Shao-ting, and Professor Yang Kuo-shu. For the Editorial Board, nine were elected, including Professor Yang Kuo-shu, Mr. Chen Shao-ting, Mr. Chen Ku-ying, and Mr. Chang Ching-hang, among others.[5]   Although the board never met, nor did it at any time guide the direction of the journal, it was a body of men and women sympathetic to the ideas of political reforms whose achievements either in academic circles or in society conferred a sense of prestige and legitimacy on the journal.

Chang Ching-hang in particular were the guiding spirits of the journal.   Mr. Chen Shao-ting and Professor Hungdah Chiu principally served as the liaison with the party, and Professor Yang Kuo-shu was in charge of editing.   In March 1971, he was publicly listed as the editor-in-chief.

The party clearly gave its approval for the merger of the three groups, though the degree to which it actively urged the merger was not known.   However, through 1971 until the early part of 1972 the ruling party kept in very close contact with the journal.   This task was entrusted to the Sixth Section of the Secretariat General, which was in charge of united front work, i.e., contact and supervision of nonparty groups and organizations.   The liaison apparently was as close as it was courteous.   From time to time, the Sixth Section would invite leading members of the journal to dinners at which views would be exchanged.   It was clear that, though the party did not formally impose a censorship, it was intensely concerned with what the journal printed.   Given the long years of experience of the party leaders in handling various groups, the young scholars must have sensed that they were placed in a most delicate situation.   The suggestions and advice given at the dinner table must have been rather difficult to resist, as they were so politely offered.

In January 1971, following the merger, articles by Professor Chen Ku-ying, Mr. Chen Shao-ting, Mr. Chang Ching-hang, and Mr. Shao Hsiang-feng appeared in the journal which took a more critical position toward the government. This action, however, immediately provoked a fairly strong reaction from some members of the journal and shattered the appearance of unity, thus presaging the division from within that was taking shape. Professor Shih Chi-yung, Professor Li Chung-hui, Professor Kuan Chung, and Mr. Yu Hseuh-min wrote a protest to the journal. Pointedly refuting the theses of the articles as exaggerated and likely to lead to misunderstandings, they requested that in the future any article, if not approved by the members of the board as a whole, not be given the imprimatur of the journal.[6] Whatever the motivations behind the protest, the letter reflected a view more to the liking of the ruling party and government.

This incipient division within the Ta-hsueh tsa-chih, however, did not deter the journal from publishing critical articles. The long essay, An Analysis of the Social Forces in Taiwan, by Chang Ching-hang and others, was published in July-September, and gave a powerful impetus to the ferment for political reforms.

In October 1971, simultaneous with publication of the program for political reform, the Ta-hsueh tsa-chih chose to republish an article by Chiang Ching-kuo written some decades before memorializing the death of a close friend during his days in Kiang-hsi.[7] This was a sentimental piece, speaking of friendship, the deceased's dedication to the reforms Chiang Ching-kuo had been trying to put into effect, and hope for the future of China. It is possible that the young university professors deemed it an inspiring piece of work; it is more likely that it was used as a reminder to Chiang Ching-kuo of his youthful days as a reformer and as a signal to him that the university professors and students still had high hopes in him. Indeed, given the highly charged political atmosphere, publication of this article led to speculations both in Taiwan and abroad. A sophisticated observer went so far as to suggest that an implicit agreement between Chiang Ching-kuo and the intellectual group had been consummated, that in return for protection and support of Chiang Ching-kuo against the attacks of others, presumably the more conservative factions in the ruling party, the journal would support Chiang Ching-kuo in his struggle for power against the older generation party leaders.[8]

This conjecture, although sophisticated, was not quite accurate. It was, of course, plausible that both the Ta-hsueh tsa-chih group and Chiang Ching-kuo were concerned with rejuvenation of the ruling stratum and the welfare of peasants and workers and that Chiang Ching-kuo might not be absolutely opposed to the activities of the young intellectuals. Yet it definitely did not follow that Chiang Ching-kuo was committed to a liberal democratic program of political reforms. During 1971-1972, Chiang Ching-kuo did, on a number of

In late 1971 and early 1972, the Ta-hsueh tsa-chih, confirmed in its position as the theoretical organ of the intellectual community, went through further expansion. For the year of 1972, eighty-five men and women in Taiwan and seventeen abroad were listed as members of the board. The publisher, manager, honorable chairman, chairman, and editor-in-chief remained unchanged, indicating a sense of continuity. The Standing Committee of the Board had seventeen members instead of the eleven it had had the previous year; and the Editorial Board listed ten in comparison to nine a year prior. [9] The dynamics also changed somewhat. A number of young university student activists were for the first time invited to participate as members of the board. Among them were Miss Chen Ling-yu, a native Taiwanese in her early twenties, president of the Student Association of the School of Law at National Taiwan University; Mr. Wang Fu-su, a medical student in his early twenties, and president of the Student Association of the university; and Mr. Hung Shan-hsiang, also a native Taiwanese, a student of law and chairman of the publication Fa Yen. All three had played a most active role in the Protect Tiao-yu-tai Movement and the ferment for political reforms. Presumably their participation was a reflection of the ferment for reforms as well as an impetus to it.

By this time, the ruling party had begun to fear that things were getting out of control, and its relations with the journal were noticeably cool and becoming more and more difficult. In February-March 1972, the party expressed great displeasure with the direction of the journal's editorial policy and demanded that it be modified or toned down. Professors Hungdah Chiu, Shih Chi-yang, and Kuan Chung, partly by conviction and partly as a reflection of the party view, threatened to withdraw from the journal and to lead others in doing so if the demand were not met. Professor Hungdah Chiu, writing in November 1971, had apparently experienced second thoughts about the ferment for political reforms. Arguing that in times of crisis the government on Taiwan deserved all-out support, he cautioned intellectuals to be careful in speech and action so that they would not increase troubles for the government or the sense of uneasiness among the people. [10]

Faced with the demand to change the editorial policy, the leading group of the journal was severely divided. Professor Chen Ku-ying severely criticized Professor Hungdah Chiu and challenged him to withdraw, making plain that the journal could do without him. Having met with resistance, Professor Hungdah Chiu and his supporters shifted their demand and insisted that Professor Yang Kuo-shu resign from his post as editor-in-chief. Mr. Chen Shao-ting also got into the act. When Professor Yang Kuo-shu suggested that, because of the dispute, it would be a good idea if he were suspended for the time being, Mr. Chen Shao-ting took it upon himself as chairman of the board to dismiss the editor-in-chief. This move did not have the support of other important members of the journal. Emergency meetings were held at which all members of the Editorial Board indicated they would resign if Professor Yang Kuo-shu was relieved of his post. Professor Chen Ku-ying was particularly firm in his rejection of the demand. Mr. Chang Ching-hang and Mr. Chang Shao-wen rushed to Tainan to see Mr. Chen Shao-ting and persuaded him to reinstate Professor Yang Kuo-shu. Although the matter eventually was laid to rest, the damage had been done. The journal was severely demoralized and its publication delayed for a month. Relations between the group and the party could not but deteriorate further. From then on the group was cut off from access to the party leaders and had to deal with functionaries at the Taiwan Garrison Command. Professor Hungdah Chiu and his supporters, though they did not withdraw from the journal, subsequently played no active role. [11]

A much more serious controversy ensued when, in the month of April, a frontal attack was made on Professor Chen Ku-ying and indirectly on the ferment for political reforms. It began when a Mr. Ku-ying[12] wrote an article in six installments in the Chung-

yang jih-pao, claiming to speak on behalf of the ordinary citizens.[13]
The article first described student riots in France in 1968, the crisis with which France was faced, and how, at the critical time,
General de Gaulle miraculously saved the day by rallying millions
of ordinary citizens--small shopkeepers, clerks, and housewives--
in support of the government.   It went on to attack a certain profes-

In Mr. Ku-ying's article, the status quo in Taiwan was described as highly satisfying: university students, workers, small
merchants, and ordinary citizens could do what they pleased and
lived fairly comfortably; they did not have to fear "class struggle"
and "labor reform," nor robbers and banditry, nor bombs and rocks
thrown by "politically conscious youth."   The criticisms of capitalists by young intellectuals were refuted on the grounds that bankers
and entrepreneurs risked their fortunes and provided jobs for the
millions; if they lived a life of luxury, they had worked for it and
deserved it.[16]   And the government, the article declared, deserved
support for its effort in "building a stable society in which people
are secure in their work and toil and can seek a happy life."[17]
The thesis of this long article could be summed up as saying that
the status quo was preferable to the dangers and risks of change,
that any student movement inevitably led to riots and instability, and
that instability led to social disintegration in times of crisis.

As a polemic, this long article was exceptionally well-written,
appealing as it did to fear of turmoil and the instinct to preserve
what has been attained.   The party organ Chung-yang jih-pao immediately issued the article in book form, endorsed it, and adver-
tised its sale.   Within a few days, it was reported that some
200,000 copies had been sold, making it the literary success of
the year, and 98 percent of the readers writing letters to the editor
of the newspaper fully supported the position of the author.[18]

It could not be denied that the tract had profoundly affected
many people with generally conservative views.   An old professor

at National Taiwan University was so impressed by the arguments that he bought copies to give his friends and students. And a certain high-ranking party official was so enthusiastic about the success of sales that he compared its value equal to an army of 200,000 men, provoking Professor Yang Kuo-shu to inquire if he was referring to an army of 200,000 men "on our side or the opposite side?"[19]

But it turned out that such success was not achieved without help from the party. Party apparatus had apparently instructed government units, universities and colleges, high schools and many private enterprises to purchase the book en masse and to distribute it to staff members and students as assigned reading; in some colleges and high schools, students were even required to write a review of the work.[20] It is an indication of the tradition of free inquiry at National Taiwan University that the students there were exempted; the administration somehow succeeded in persuading the party authority that this sort of thing could not be done.

Nevertheless, for a few days, the university professors and students were put on the defensive. It appeared that the party and government might call a halt to the ferment for political reforms. However, this did not happen. A meeting of the editorial board of the Ta-hsueh tsa-chih was convened on April 19 to discuss the issue. In addition to the editorial board, a number of students and professors, including Professor Hu Fu and this writer, were invited to participate. The discussion was rather heated. The consensus was that the attack should be faced, though how to proceed was not very clear.[21]

On April 28, a letter to the editor appeared in the Lien-ho pao severely criticizing Mr. Ku-ying for opposing reforms on the pretense of seeking progress in stability and casting doubt on the sincerity and patriotism of university professors and students.[22] Since the writer of this letter was none other than Professor Lin Chi-tung of National Taiwan University, a grand justice of the Judicial Yuan and the grandson of the national hero of the Opium War, Commissioner Lin Tse-hsu, the letter had a great effect on the morale of the young intellectuals, encouraging them to hold firm in their convictions. However, Professor Lin Chi-tung was made to pay a high price for speaking his mind; anonymous, unfriendly telephone calls were made to him and his personal conduct was maliciously slan-

dered by unknown sources. After the publication of this letter the
Lien-ho pao also received warning, supposedly from the highest par-
ty authorities, not to further involve the paper in the dispute over
Mr. Ku-ying's views.

On May 2, the Student Association of the Law College of Na-

[illegible faded text]

the classroom windows, straining themselves to hear the discussion.
A number of foreigners, possibly American visiting scholars and
students, also came, some of whom appeared to take notes.

The atmosphere was highly exciting. Professor Wang Wen-
hsin was the first to speak. He dwelled upon the distinction between
the student movement and riots and argued forcefully that the student
movement was needed for social reforms and progress.[23] This
writer commented on the distinctions between expert knowledge and
judgement on public affairs, affirming that, in contrast to what Mr.
Ku-ying had to say, university students definitely could and should
judge public acts; furthermore, political stability should not be con-
fused with political stagnation and political stability should imply the
ability of the political system to adapt to changes. He warned that
to endorse the thesis of Ku-ying would be self-defeating, as it would
doubtless lead to demoralization and alienation in Taiwan, as well
as unfavorable reactions abroad.[24]

Then it was Professor Wang Shao-po's turn. As usual he spoke
passionately and eloquently, delivering a long speech that took more
than an hour. He attacked the article from the perspective of Dr.
Sun Yat-sen's teachings, condemning it as violating the Three People's
Principles and refuting the thesis point by point. In particular, he
drew upon Dr. Sun Yat-sen's views on the student movement, national sovereignty, popular authority, control of the capitalist class,
and social justice.[25] The audience was visibly moved. Professor
Wang Shao-po's speech was a brilliant stroke. He had defended the

student movement with the party's rhetoric. Given the claim of the Nationalist Party and government as instruments of Dr. Sun Yat-sen's teachings, it would be impossible to attack him. The students began to join in. And Professor Chen Ku-ying, by acclamation, was invited to speak. He reiterated his view on the student movement and took the Chung-yang jih-pao to task for distortion of public opinion in its report of readers' reactions to the article. The debate among students holding different opinions became heated; a few argued that Mr. Ku-ying should be given his due, while the bulk were plainly hostile to his thesis. The meeting drew to an end.

The next day, Professor Sun Chen and this writer were invited to take part with two editors from Chung-yang jih-pao in a forum on Diversity and Alienation in the Complex Society, sponsored by the History Club of National Taiwan University. The club had hoped that the discussion would move beyond the issues posed by Mr. Ku-ying and focus on the rapidly changing society on Taiwan. However, because the student audience was still very much agitated about the work and the two editors were responsible for its publication and promotion, the discussion inevitably centered again on Ku-ying.

The newspaper editors, Mr. Lu Hsiang-shan and Mr. Tang Chu-kuo, were courteous and frank in their presentation. They related why the article by Ku-ying was chosen, explaining that given the painful experiences of the student movement in mainland China during the period of civil war and their knowledge of the Communist practice of using students for their political purposes, they were disposed favorably towards Ku-ying's perspectives and arguments. They also dwelt at some length on the danger of Communist infiltration in Taiwan, citing Chinese Communist activities in Japan to support their case. The discussion never quite came to focus on the complex society. Professor Sun Chen talked about the necessity of moving beyond the past, and the price that must be paid if progress were to be made. This writer urged the press to inform the public accurately so that the people could learn about politics and make sound political judgements. On the whole, the discussion was desultory. Again, a few students were sympathetic to the opinions of Ku-ying, while most of them were antagonistic. Many criticized the editors for supporting such a backward-looking position in a time of crisis when the ruling party and government were supposedly committed to political reforms.[26]

By this time, the public and the intellectual community had begun to react. Letters criticizing Ku-ying began to appear in newspapers. The May issue of the Ta-hseuh tsa-chih devoted a great part of the journal to articles and letters commenting on Ku-ying, including Professor Lin Chi-tung's interview with the editor of the Fa Yen Journal, the speeches by Professor Wang Wen-hsin, Profes-

taken as presenting the view of the intellectuals most succinctly.
In the first letter, he contrasted two types of mentality: escapist, conservative, and backward-looking vs. progressive, reformist, and forward-looking, or as he put it, traditionalist and soft-minded vs. modernistic and tough-minded. He affirmed his faith in a "comprehensive" modernization as the only hope of competing with the Chinese Communists: "In keeping with the trend of our time toward modernization, we must not only concern ourselves with modernization of politics, economics, and material life; we must also emphasize modernization of ideas, thoughts, values, behaviors, style and institutions so that we can aspire to build a genuine democratic, free, law-abiding, wealthy and just society."[27] In his second letter, he reiterated the view that the idealism of youth should be particularly nurtured, and youth should be respected and trusted.[28]

In Chinese intellectual communities abroad, Professor Yang Kuo-shu's opinions were cited time and again with approval, while Ku-ying was condemned as propagating a defeatist philosophy.[29] The party's attempt to dampen the enthusiasm for political reforms, it would seem, had backfired.

In the aftermath of this controversy, a calmness descended. In the summer, Professor Chen Ku-ying, due to psychological exhaustion from having had to defend himself against attack, decided that he would like to take a trip to the United States. It was widely assumed that the government would not let him go, but instead he was encouraged to do so. Leaving Taiwan in the latter part of July, he travelled widely on the continent; and given his reputation as a well-known intellectual from Taiwan, he was warmly welcomed by Chinese intellectuals in the States. He talked and lectured to Chinese student groups both in California and New York, including many pro-Peking groups. It appeared that the security organs in Taiwan had anticipated such a contingency; yet they had not posed any objections except to make the peculiar suggestion that they would like to be informed of his contacts abroad so that he would not be accused of pro-Communist sentiments. It is not known if Professor Chen Ku-ying acquiesced.

After touring the United States for a couple of weeks, Professor Chen Ku-ying seriously entertained the idea of spending a year or two in America doing research on Chinese philosophy. He approached a number of universities and was fairly well-received; a research position seemed to be forthcoming. However, while he was visiting Chicago word came from Taiwan that his detractors were again attacking him, accusing him this time of having plagiarized Chinese Communist sources in his studies of Lao Tzu and demanding that he be removed from his position at National Taiwan University. To defend his reputation and integrity, Professor Chen Ku-ying abruptly returned to Taiwan in August.[30]

After his return, Professor Chen Ku-ying became actively involved in the debate on nationalism then going on at National Taiwan University. As indicated above, he and Professor Wang Shao-po argued forcefully on behalf of militant nationalism and condemned the influences of imperialism, in particular the influence of the United States and Japan. In a heated exchange in the forum on nationalism, he publicly accused a student in his department of being a secret agent of the security organs. This unfortunate incident created a controversy, making his position at the university quite untenable. It appeared that he had, to some degree, redefined his position towards the West and his views of democracy and freedom, presumably as a result of his exposure and contact with Chinese intellectual groups of different political persuasions in the United States. Clearly, the controversy he had created and his posture did not endear him to the ruling party and government.

Reactions soon followed. In early February 1973, during the university recess, Professor Chen Ku-ying, along with Professor Wang Shao-po and a number of students at National Taiwan University and Cheng Kung College, was suddenly arrested by the Taiwan Garrison Command.[31] An official of the Secretariat General of the ruling party stated that the professors and students had organized "reading clubs" devoted to the study of Chinese Communist literature, in particular the works of Mao Tse-tung, and that they had planned to expand their group and influence in Taiwan. It was also

[illegible faded text]

and borrowed by Professor Chen Ku-ying.[34] At any rate, due to the efforts of the president of National Taiwan University and the China Youth Corps, the detained professors were released after twenty-four hours, on promise of good behavior, and the students after four or five days. Before the students' release, a friend of theirs publicly slashed his neck and wrote a letter of protest with his blood.[35]

After the incident, Professor Chen Ku-ying was relieved of his position at National Taiwan University and given a job as a researcher at the International Relations Institution, a research organization closely related to the party and government. It could be assumed that he would not be doing much except drawing pay to support himself and his family. Neither he nor Professor Wang Shao-po have since published any article or given any speech. In short, they were effectively silenced.

At about the same time, rumors began to circulate at National Taiwan University that Professor Hu Fu and Professor Yang Kuo-shu were also personae non grata, implying that they too would be removed from their teaching positions. Although this did not materialize, they felt threatened. Professor Yang Kuo-shu had already resigned from the position of editor-in-chief of the Ta-hseuh tsachih, and the editorial board was dissolved due to lack of leadership. Mr. Chang Ching-hang, having been implicated in the case of Professors Chen Ku-ying and Wang Shao-po, was compelled to resign from the Secretariat General of the Nationalist Party. It is not known if he was also expelled from the party.

Under these circumstances, the university professors and students were severely demoralized, frustrated, and fearful of further reprisals. The future of the Ta-hsueh tsa-chih was in doubt. Among the core group, only Mr. Chen Shao-ting and Mr. Chang Ching-hang were actively in charge of the journal.

In the March-April issue, writing in an editorial, Mr. Chang Ching-hang openly related that those involved with the journal had seriously thought of suspending its publication. "These days, due to various objective factors, we feel both physically and psychologically exhausted and demoralized; thus, the publication of this issue has been delayed. . . . We have reflected seriously if indeed the efforts we have made in the past few years have influenced adversely the security of society and hurt our nation's long-range interests and opportunity for survival. If the answer is affirmative, this definitely was not our original intention. Since the answer is difficult to come by, we do not deny that we have seriously thought of suspension. . . ."[36] Again, "Truth cannot be monopolized by the minority; right and wrong must be decided by the majority of the people. We openly state that in our opinion, the ruling party and government on the one hand and society and the intellectual community on the other still hold very different views as to the future of our nation and the course of action that should be pursued. As to what path we should take and how we should go about it, we sincerely hope our readers will point the way for us."[37]

This painful, open soul-searching and pleading for moral support from readers solicited an immediate response. Telephone calls and letters poured in from readers in Taiwan and the United States, urging the journal to persevere in the face of difficulty. A university student wrote that "the journal should not suspend itself; it could only be closed by the government."[38] A second reader urged the journal to keep on struggling at any cost: "If the journal is closed, it would show how weak and pitiful the forces for social justice are in our society. . . . What we need most at this time is the moral courage as you have shown. . . ."[39] A third reader, apparently satirically, argued for suspension of the journal so that it could escape government persecution.[40]

While the response of the readers was gratifying, the prospects were grim. In a supreme effort, the journal in May 1973 committed itself to what was referred to as a "new effort." "For more than a year, the reform movement initiated by the government has been vigorously moving forward, and the effort our journal had made in promoting participation of citizens in the affairs of the state has also come to an end. . . . We aspire from now on to move into a new stage and dedicate ourselves to a new effort. . . . We hope that through the participation of our readers we can promote a mean-

ocean, as well as communities for the aged from wealthy societies in the West, did not provoke any favorable response.[42] It was, on the contrary, criticized by the Chinese intellectual community in the United States as advocating "modernization" in the narrowest sense of the word and modeling itself on "capitalism."[43]

Furthermore, at this time Mr. Chang Ching-hang was already contemplating taking part in the December elections for the City Council of Taipei and could not devote himself to the work of the journal. Indeed, there were signs that the journal was drifting; the drive and confidence of the previous years were things of the past.

In the elections for the City Council of Taipei, the ruling party was severely challenged by Chang Ching-hang and his supporters. Following ten days of campaigning as stipulated by election regulations, the elections were held on December 1, 1973. Altogether, sixty-five candidates competed for forty-nine seats. Of the candidates, forty-five were nominated by the ruling party.[44] Mr. Chang Ching-hang, campaigning as an independent since he had left the Secretariat General of the ruling party, asserted forcefully his qualifications to take part in politics. Presenting himself as the editor of Ta-hsueh tsa-chih and citing his visit to the United States at the invitation of the State Department, he stated that he was dedicated to the reform program of the journal, and urged youth to work with him in building a new society.[45] To strengthen his position, he and a number of other candidates organized themselves into a United Independent Front and ran on a common platform highly critical of the government.[46] They urged the "opening up" of the ruling apparatus and the adoption of "rule by law instead of rule by men." The posts of the governor of Taiwan and the mayor of Taipei, they argued, should be made elective rather than appointive; and the central government should govern through legislation rather than by executive order.[47] Although they claimed that the United Independent Front was solely aimed at "mutual security" and was not an opposition party, the challenge could not but pose a dilemma for the ruling elite.

The organizer and leader of the United Independent Front was Mr. Kang Ning-hsiang, a young native Taiwanese with a power base in the Wan-hwa area of Taipei who had just recently been elected to the Legislative Yuan in the supplementary elections. He was, by all accounts, rapidly rising as a powerful politician with a bright future. His brother, Kang Yi-hsiang, was competing in the elections for the City Council of Taipei. In the heat of the campaign the group got hold of and made public a secret document drafted by the Social Work Committee of the Central Committee of the ruling party. Entitled "Report on Social Conditions in the City of Taipei," it was an analysis, district by district, of the strengths and weaknesses of the party and its opponents, with references to large groups of men and women designated as "deviationists," that is, hostile to the party and needing to be closely watched. It also urged party members to exert an utmost effort in the elections so that party victory would be insured.[48] The United Independent Front's publication of this document, with sarcastic comments, could not but embarrass and anger the party leadership. Many old party functionaries at the Secretariat General of the ruling party were particularly critical of Mr. Chang Ching-hang, accusing him of being "ungrateful" and "biting the hand that feeds him."

In another campaign pamphlet, Mr. Chang Ching-hang went all out to defend himself against the insinuation that he was sympathetic to the Taiwanese Independence Movement, making his relationship with the party even more antagonistic. He argued that if the Taiwanese Independence Movement were interpreted as a movement for sovereignty and autonomy from Chinese Communist rule, then he could not see anything wrong with that; were not the efforts of the Nationalist Party for the past two decades aimed precisely at maintaining autonomy from the Chinese Communists? If the movement were referred to as a civil rights movement for the Taiwanese people, comparable to the civil rights movement in the United States, he was in favor of it. Only if the movement were interpreted as a violent revolutionary movement to overthrow the government was he against it. His participation in the elections, he asserted, should be proof enough that he would not have anything to do with revolution.[49]

A few days before the elections, the front was dealt a setback when a member of the group, Mr. Wei Yi-min, appeared to have

true that his strategy had alienated many of his colleagues at the Ta-hsueh tsa-chih: they complained that he was quite prepared to use his connections with the journal for his own political gains, a tactic which they saw as short-sighted; furthermore, they considered his attempt to capitalize on his visit to the United States through the invitation of the Department of State to be in poor taste. His cooperation with other independent candidates of inferior qualifications and moral character such as Mr. Wei Yi-min had also hurt his chances. Nevertheless, since he had been given a more than fair chance to win, rumors circulated that the party had used any and all means to defeat him, including the free use of bribery to buy votes, giving army men leave to return to their domiciles to vote for party nominees, and manipulating the counting of votes.

After the election, Mr. Chang Ching-hang was left a bitter and demoralized man. More importantly, the Ta-hsueh tsa-chih was now in disarray. By this time the ferment for political reforms had, for all practical purposes, come to an end.

Although the ferment had subsided, some of its aftermath was still to be faced. In the spring of 1974, the Department of Philosophy at National Taiwan University was again involved in a controversy which tore the department apart and culminated in a massive shake-up of personnel. A central figure in the controversy was the newly appointed department chairman, Dr. Sun Chih-yen. Opposing him were Professors Wang Shao-po, Chou Tien-yi, Lin Chen-hung, and their student supporters. Professor Chen Chung-ying, a former department chairman and professor at the City University of New York in the United States, was also implicated. In an emergency meeting of the department, Dr. Sun Chih-yen accused his opponents of propagating Chinese Communist thought and taking the thought of Mao Tse-tung as the correct line in philosophical work. He charged them with having connections with "liberal" American professors and dedicating themselves to infiltrating National Taiwan University in preparation for a Communist take-over. Though Dr. Sun Chih-yen presented himself as a lone crusader fighting for the integrity of the university and for sovereignty of the Republic of China from interference from without, he indicated that he had been given full power and support from "above" to reorganize the department when he took over as chairman. He demanded that the department be purified of undesirable faculty. [51]

When, during the summer, rumors began to circulate that a "purge" was going to take place, the Dean of Humanities, the Chairman of the History Department, the Chairman of the Foreign Literature Department, and many other professors paid a visit to the president of the university, Dr. Yen Chen-hsing, and expressed their opposition to any such drastic action. The president was noncommittal; he explained that "pressures from without" were very severe, but he would do his best to see to it that as few as possible were dismissed. Nevertheless, the results proved that he did give in to outside pressures. Four professors were dismissed, including Professor Wang Shao-po and the former chairman, Professor Chou Tien-yi; two others, including Professor Lin Chen-hung, were put on probationary status.

While Dr. Sun Chih-yen emerged as the victor, it appeared that he was not necessarily the originator of the move. More likely he was the front man. Although personality conflict and department issues no doubt played a part, the en masse dismissal at National Taiwan University must have been recognized on all sides as a very crucial decision; and Dr. Sun Chih-yen was hardly the man to take upon himself such a heavy responsibility. The "pressures from without" referred to by President Yen Chen-hsing could only have come from the party.

In a broad sense, this move against selected young professors could be seen as a sequel to the ferment for political reforms, a deliberate move to settle old scores. [52]   Clearly the intellectual group committed to basic political change was again on the defensive.

IV. THE PARTY AND GOVERNMENT REFORM MEASURES

Two days after the expulsion of the Republic of China from the United Nations, the party leadership met in emergency meetings and pledged to proceed with political reforms. The assumption of gov-

task facing them was that of "survival." [...] to compete with Peking for power, they argued that by opting for a "democratic and free way of life," i.e., siding with the United States in the world arena while simultaneously "preserving the Chinese tradition" and pushing on vigorously with economic development and social welfare, they could not only remain undefeated but could seriously aspire to influence the development of China in the future. The cherished goal of "retaking mainland China" was for all practical purposes given up. [2]

Broadly speaking, the reform measures adopted by the party and government in 1972-1973 could be grouped under five headings. First, the government expanded the popular base of the people's representative organs by enlarging the National Assembly, the Legislative Yuan, and the Control Yuan through supplementary election and presidential appointment. Second, to revitalize the party and government, more "young men of talent" and native Taiwanese were recruited into the decision-making echelon. Third, to rectify the work of the government, the administration was made more open and accessible to the people, strict personal behaviors were prescribed for bureaucrats, and an effort was initiated to curb corruption. Fourth, to seek the support of youth, closer contact between youth and government was encouraged, and aid was given to diverse categories of youth to help them in career planning and studies. And fifth, to succor the peasants and workers, agricultural modernization was pushed and more attention paid to the social welfare of the poor.

Since many if not all of these reform measures had been demanded by the young intellectuals, it could be assumed that their ferment for political reforms brought about results. However, it can hardly be argued that the ruling elite had committed itself to democratic politics or that it had gone out of its way to protect and promote human rights and individual freedoms. The selective reprisals against individual professors and students would testify to the limits beyond which challenge to authorities would not be tolerated. Moreover, many other reform measures proposed by university professors and students were ignored and those reform measures adopted, such as strengthening the people's representative organs, recruiting young men of talent, and promoting the social welfare of peasants and workers, definitely did not go as far as the intellectuals had proposed, as will be shown. Taken as a whole, the reform measures emphasized specific policy choices and administrative innovations, and fell considerably short of the basic reforms demanded by the intellectuals. To put it another way, the ruling elite was quite prepared to accommodate the young university professors and students to a certain degree, but at the same time was adamant in holding to its basic political values and power structure.

While it was not possible to assess the reforms with any finality, as the effort was still going on and new reform measures could still have been adopted, it was definitely premature to suggest that the assumption of governmental power by Chiang Ching-kuo and those reform measures accompanying that act ushered in a new era of politics on Taiwan, a new era "of political rationality, of populist spirit, and of political benevolence."[3]

The reform measures relating to the people's representative organs were decided upon in early 1972. From February 20 to March 25, 1972, the National Assembly met and, among other things, opted for supplementary elections. From the very beginning, the chance for complete reelection of the three bodies of the people's representative organs were slim indeed. The experience of the 1969 supplementary elections pointed to the need for some kind of compromise. From the perspective of the ruling elite, the dilemma in 1972 just as in 1969 was surely that of legitimacy. President Chiang Kai-shek, both in his speech to the National Assembly and in a speech at the Third Plenum of the Central Committee of the ruling party, reaffirmed that the government was based on constitutional rule and derived its authority from the National Assembly.[4] With such emphasis on the continuity of constitutional rule, it could hardly be expected that the party and government would contemplate drastic changes in the people's representative organs. The decision of the party leadership, following discussion at the Third Plenum of the Central Committee, was pre-

~~sented to the National Assembly as a resolution for revision of the~~

face election at the end of their terms according to constitutional provisions.[5]

The intents of this proposal were clear. The principle of legitimacy was upheld, as the party saw it, and the interests of the original members of the three bodies would not be adversely affected. However, the phrase "the next term" used in referring to the exercise of power and functions of the original members provoked a great deal of confusion. The Ta-hsueh tsa-chih group took it to indicate that the ruling elite had moved closer to their position of complete reelection of the people's representatives and complained bitterly when it turned out otherwise.[6] On the other hand, members of the National Assembly maneuvered strenuously for removal of the phrase, so that no ambiguity would remain as to their life tenure. After three days of heated discussion and maneuvering, the phrase was deleted from the adopted resolution, with Ko Cheng-kang explaining that he had never intended it to mean very much. Thus, with only minor changes in wording, the decision of the party leadership was given approval by the National Assembly.[7] This episode, comical as it was, tells a great deal about the political climate of that period.

On June 29 the President promulgated the regulations governing the coming supplementary elections. This was a complex set of rules dealing with the number of additional members, the electors, the candidates, the election organs, etc.[8] All told, 119 new

members would be added to the three bodies of the people's representative organs; among them, 23 were to be elected by the membership of various vocational, professional, and women's groups,
and 20 overseas Chinese were to be appointed by the President. [9]

Reaction to the decision on supplementary elections and the
regulations was mixed. [10] Many young intellectuals were disillu-
sioned that no more new members would be elected, as they had
apparently been led to expect a larger number. [11] Moreover, there
was widespread skepticism that the ruling party would conduct an
open and fair election. As to specific points, presidential appointment from overseas Chinese communities came in for criticism as
it was feared that those appointed would not be suitable, and that
those suitable would not or could not accept the appointment. [12]
Assignment of quotas to vocational, professional, and women's associations was condemned on the grounds that it was a backward
method, long rendered useless by a complex and rapidly changing
society. [13] Also, objections were raised over the fact that the regulations were not enacted by the Legislative Yuan but were promulgated by the President; and the fact that the rights of candidates to
compete could be deprived by administrative decisions without due
process of law was censured as violating the constitution. [14]

The party leadership took the approaching elections seriously.
Through the fall of 1972, it time and again gave solemn promise
that the party nomination would be guided by the principle of selecting the best candidates, that nonparty candidates would be encouraged to compete, and that the elections would be conducted fairly. [15]
To some extent, the party nominees were an improvement over
things in the past. More youth and women were nominated, and native Taiwanese accounted for a fairly high percentage. Moreover,
in a number of electoral districts the ruling party either did not
nominate any candidate or nominated fewer candidates than the number of seats in contest, so that nonparty candidates would be assured of success. [16]

As election time approached, Taipei was buzzing with political
activity. Notwithstanding the promise of the ruling party, the nonparty candidates were as vigilant as they were bold. In late October, in a meeting held in Taipei and attended by more than one
hundred potential candidates and their supporters from all over Taiwan, a resolution was adopted charging the ruling party with tam-

pering with ballots in past elections and calling for strict enforcement of election laws this time. The leaders of the group, presumably Mr. Kang Ning-hsiang and Huang Hsin-chieh, both politicians with their power base in Taipei, insisted that they did not
plan to organize an opposition party, that their aim was only to
help the government achieve the goal of strengthening democratic
[17]

cinct.[18] A week later some eighty nonparty candidates formally
announced that they would ignore government regulations restricting
their campaign practices.[19] In particular, they were irked by
rules specifying that campaign speeches could be delivered only at
certain government-sponsored forums unless two-thirds of the candidates in the district agreed otherwise.[20]

Against this background of challenge and threat of boycott, the
elections were duly held in late December 1972. The ruling party,
as anticipated, performed very well indeed, if judged only by the
returns. All told, 53 new members were elected to the National
Assembly, and 36 to the Legislative Yuan. Of the former, eight
were women; of the latter, five were women. The average age of
new members of the National Assembly was 45.58 years old; of the
Legislative Yuan, 47.36. The educational level of the new members
was appreciably higher, with four doctoral recipients in the National
Assembly and six in the Legislative Yuan. The ruling party succeeded in capturing 43 of the 53 seats in the National Assembly and
30 of the 36 in the Legislative Yuan.[21]

A week later, the President announced his selection of fifteen
new members of the Legislative Yuan, along with five new members
of the Control Yuan, from the overseas Chinese communities. They
were, on the whole, older and established leaders of their communities with ties to the Nationalist Party.[22] Rumors previously circulated that some young scholars abroad, such as Dr. Hungdah Chiu,
would be appointed to serve were proved false.

In the latter part of February 1973, the election of additional members of the Control Yuan was held in Taiwan. All seven candidates of the ruling party were elected; thirteen nonparty candidates were defeated, with Mr. Chen Shao-ting getting one vote and the others getting none at all.[23]

As anticipated, the ruling party and government reacted most favorably to the election results. Premier Chiang Ching-kuo declared it a great success, hailing it as "a symbol of the trust of the people in the government to maintain constitutional rule."[24] Many a defeated nonparty candidate, and the intellectual community as a whole, however, tended to take a more somber view. In a forum sponsored by the Ta-hsueh tsa-chih to review the elections, many criticisms were voiced against the Nationalist Party and its conduct in the elections.[25] For many former candidates, the bitterest complaints were directed at the restrictions on their campaign activities, the aid of the ruling party to its nominees, diverse sorts of fraudulent manipulation of election results, and bribery.[26] Mr. Bruce Jacobs, the only foreign participant in the forum, referred to some of these criticisms. He suggested that the elections had not been as open and fair as the government had promised, given the discrepancy in resources between KMT candidates and their opponents and the restrictions of campaign activities which favored the ruling party nominees.[27] He made the interesting observation that the government had promised to "win the heart of the people rather than their votes" but had achieved neither. In every forum during the campaign, he said, the independent candidates invariably attacked the ruling party in order to gain voters' sympathy; yet the Nationalist Party nominees rarely, if ever, gave the impression that they deemed their party membership an honor and never defended the party's honor. Obviously the party had not won the hearts of the people; otherwise, the tactics of the nonparty candidates should have provoked an adverse reaction from voters.[28]

More significantly, the need for an opposition party was again posed at the forum. Both Mr. Chang Tah-ming, a young lawyer, and Professor Su Tsun-hsiang, commented on what they saw as the key to an open and fair election: that an opposition party was needed to check the power of the ruling party. As Professor Su Tsun-hsiang put it: "Besides a high degree of political ethics and maturity in style, the most important and basic condition of democratic politics is a healthy party politics. If there was not an outside force to supervise it, and if it were only dependent on the open-mindedness of a powerful ruling party, progress towards democratic politics would be very difficult. In my opinion, the question that anyone concerned with democratic politics, either in the party or without, should give serious thought to is how to nurture a moderate and legitimate opposition party."[29]

stage of learning how to use the democratic system."[30] Elections within this framework did not have anything to do with changing political regimes, the editorial claimed; rather, the meaning of elections lay in that they served the function of communication between the ruling party and the people and provided a vehicle through which talented men and women were recruited into governmental services. The ruling party, it went on to say, should realize that winning the people's hearts was more crucial than winning votes and was the only way the regime could be consolidated. To achieve this goal, concluded the editorial, the ruling party must modernize itself and set a good example for the operation of a party system; only thus could it lead China into a new era of democracy.[31]

In addition to broadening the base of the three representative bodies at the national level, the ruling party moved to incorporate "young men of talent" in the decision-making echelon. The assumption of governmental power by Chiang Ching-kuo, no doubt, was the cornerstone of efforts to revitalize the ruling elite. However, the influence of traditional political culture was such that his advent to power was done in a most circuitous fashion. After the election of Chiang Kai-shek to the fifth term of presidency and Yen Chia-kan to the vice-presidency, Mr. Yen Chia-kan resigned from his post of premiership and recommended Chiang Ching-kuo to take his place. In a letter to the President, couched in the incredibly ornate style of the traditional literati-official, he suggested that he would like to devote all his time and energy to the vice-presidency and recommended Chiang Ching-kuo as the most ideal candidate for the premiership. Chiang Ching-kuo was praised for his personal qualities, his performance, and his contributions to the party and nation. [32] The Standing Committee of the Central Committee, as expected, concurred with this recommendation, and petitioned Chiang Kai-shek, in his position as the director general of the party, to draft Chiang Ching-kuo as premier. [33] After a suitable interval, Chiang Kai-shek agreed to the recommendation, and with the approval of the Legislative Yuan, Chiang Ching-kuo was appointed as premier.

With the appointment of Chiang Ching-kuo, speculation centered on his selection of a new cabinet which he announced in the latter part of May. To a degree he succeeded in giving a new image to the government. A number of younger men and native Taiwanese were recruited into the government. Of the 23 cabinet members, 13 were new appointees and 6 native Taiwanese. The average age was 61.99, two years younger than the average in 1970. Of the new appointees, 9 were below age 60, the youngest one being 49. Moreover, the post of vice-premier which Chiang Ching-kuo had held for years was given to a Taiwanese, Mr. Hsu Ching-chung, as were the positions of Minister of the Interior and Minister of Communication. [34] Mr. Kao Yu-shu, the newly appointed Minister of Communication, was a well-known politician with connections abroad, particularly in the United States and Japan, and a substantial power base in Taiwan.

On the subcabinet level, a number of young men with good academic backgrounds were appointed. Among them, Mr. Frederich Chen, age 37, Ph.D. from Yale University and director of the American Affairs Department of the Foreign Ministry, was given the post of director of the Government Information Office. Professor Liang Shang-yung, 40, Ph.D. from the University of Missouri and a dean of National Chengchi University, was appointed the vice-minister of the Ministry of Education; and Professor Liu Fei-lung, in his forties, Ph.D. from National Chengchi University, was appointed vice-minister of the Ministry of the Interior.

For the position of governor of Taiwan, Chiang Ching-kuo chose Mr. Hsieh Tung-min, a native Taiwanese with long years of experience in party and government affairs. The post of the mayor of Taipei, which was directly governed by the Executive Yuan, was given to Mr. Chang Feng-shu, a native Taiwanese in his early forties, and magistrate of Pingtung Hsien from 1964-1972.[35] The appointment of Chang Feng-shu, and to a lesser degree that of Kao Yu-shu, were taken as indications that Chiang Ching-kuo was serious in working together with younger native Taiwanese politicians.

The significance of the new cabinet was duly noted by the intellectual community and society at large. An editorial in the Ta- [illegible]

[illegible] Committee of the ruling party was reorganized. On the whole the break with the past was of modest degree, as the secretary general and many party leaders were retained. However, some changes were made. The main thrust of the reorganization was simplification of structure and recruitment of young men of talent. As Secretary General Chang Pao-shu explained it, the goals were to streamline the apparatus, to concentrate power, and to use new and talented party cadres. Men of talent, experience, and academic background, he stated, were selected to serve, and young promising and loyal party cadres were promoted without regard to their ranks.[37]

The functional units of the Central Committee were reduced from 16 to 12, and committees were substituted for the divisional structure used in previous years. Clearly the committee structure was judged more flexible and better able to absorb young men and native Taiwanese. Two native Taiwanese, Mr. Lin Chin-sheng and Mr. Lai Shun-sheng, were given the high posts of deputy secretary general and head of the Secretariat General respectively. Also a new Committee on Youth Work was created, to which Professor Wang Wei-lung, 38, a Ph.D. in physics trained in the United States, was appointed. This was an indication of Chiang Ching-kuo's stress on youth work. Professor Wang Wei-lung's family connection with the party and his youth had no doubt contributed to his selection.[38]

A year later, in June 1973, the policy of recruiting men and women of talent into government service was given a further impetus. Dr. Hsu Hsien-hsiu, the president of Tsing Hua University, succeeded Dr. Wu Ta-yu as chairman of the National Science Council, while Dr. Wu Ta-yu retained his post as chairman of the Committee of Science Development of the National Security Council. Dr. Hsu Hsien-hsiu, a scientist by training, was well-known for his administrative skill and his stress on scientific development to meet social needs. His assumption of the new position pointed to a close relationship between scientific research and defense efforts and the economic development of Taiwan.[39] Dr. Robert Lee, 50, a staff member of the Sino-American Joint Committee on Rural Reconstruction, replaced retiring Dr. T. H. Shen as its chairman.[40] Moreover, the Council of International Economic Cooperation and Development was succeeded by the Economic Planning Committee, charged exclusively with long-term planning. Dr. Phillip Chang, vice-chairman and secretary-general of the council was named to head the commission. To aid him, Professor Kuo Wan-yung, a native Taiwanese, and Professor Sun Chen were appointed vice-chairmen of the commission. A third professor of economics from National Taiwan University, Dr. Liang Kuo-shu, also a native Taiwanese, was given the post of vice-chairman of the Commission of Research, Development and Evaluation of the Executive Yuan.[41]

This series of appointments recruited many "young men of talent" and native Taiwanese. Experienced administrators with competent academic backgrounds accounted for a high percentage of the new appointees. In a sense, it could be argued that the recommendation to use technocrats had been heeded, particularly in the domains of economic development and science. However, there was a discernible pattern of selection. On the whole, young men and women recruited into government service were the "cautious, subservient, and conservative" type.[42] Few of them were known for forcefulness in expressing their opinions. With the exception of Professor Sun Chen, none of them had taken part in the intellectual ferment for political reforms; and none of them had criticized the party and government publicly. Well-known young intellectuals such as Professor Hu Fu, Professor Yang Kuo-shu, and Mr. Chang Ching-hang had not been recruited. Moreover, it was difficult to judge the degree to which these "young men of talent" were given decision-making power and their opinions and recommendations were taken seriously. In other words, the recruitment of "young men of talent" was not implemented without strings attached.

Immediately after his appointment to the premiership and his selection of the cabinet, Chiang Ching-kuo moved to make the gov-

ernment more open and accessible to the people, to curb the bureaucracy, and to extirpate corruption. Quite deliberately he made himself highly visible. He talked to government officials[43] and youth
groups,[44] exhorting, cajoling, and encouraging them; he took inspection tours, visiting the remote rural areas and fishery villages;[45]
and he wrote letters to government officials, giving detailed instruc-

at all levels rules for conducting government business, as well as
personal behavior. Emphasis was placed on austerity and getting
things done. According to the program, building of offices and
other projects by the government at all levels, if not already bud-
geted, should be discontinued. Ground-breaking and dedication ceremonies for public projects should be eliminated. Foreign travel
and participation in international conferences by government officials
should be tightly controlled and participants carefully selected. Inspection tours by government officials should be reduced to an absolute minimum, no inspection group should accept any entertainment, and in no case should students be assigned to welcoming ceremonies. Heads-of-ministries and government officials at all levels,
apart from taking part in government-sponsored dinners and parties,
should not entertain guests and visitors and should decline any invitations to parties. Government officials should not lavishly entertain and solicit gifts at weddings and funerals. Government officials
at all levels should not patronize night clubs, bars, dancing halls,
and "hostess" restaurants. All heads of government offices should
decline invitations for opening ceremonies and ribbon-cuttings of all
kinds. Overtime pay and travel allowances in the budget of government units should not be used for any other purposes. In conducting
public business, government officials should be responsible, and
finally, unnecessary meetings should not be held, problems should
be dealt with without delay, and action should be taken without pro-
crastination.[48]

This set of instructions, coming at a time when Chiang Ching-
kuo had just assumed government leadership, and reflecting to a

substantial degree the people's complaints against the bureaucrats, created a sensation in Taiwan. Ministers and members of the cabinet pledged themselves to comply and set an example.[49] So did the armed forces,[50] the Provincial government of Taiwan,[51] and various social organizations.[52] The newspapers also reacted favorably. An editorial in the Chung-yang jih-pao hailed it as the beginning of political reforms.[53] Nevertheless, some wits in Taipei dubbed it the Ten Commandments, expressing a sense of skepticism.

The government genuinely made a serious effort to implement and enforce the program. In particular the prohibition against government officials patronizing night clubs, dancing halls, and "hostess" restaurants was enforced with a vigilance rarely seen. For some two or three weeks following the announcement of the program, rumors circulated in Taipei that policemen kept under surveillance all the night clubs and other entertainment establishments throughout Taiwan, checked identifications, and recorded the names of any government officials present. A number of low-ranking government officials were dismissed from their positions due to violations of this particular injunction, and a fairly high-ranking official in the Ministry of the Interior was fired for extravagant entertainment at the wedding of his son.[54] Although after a while the enforcement appeared to slacken, there were signs that government officials were more cautious about giving the impression that they were living a life of conspicuous consumption. The business of night clubs, dancing halls, bars, and "hostess" restaurants appeared to be hurt.

In January 1973, the Executive Yuan adopted a new procedure on petitioning the government for "protection of people's rights and interests."[55] Among other things, it aimed at making it easier for the people to petition for any violation of their rights by government functionaries, and to make suggestions for reform measures. Any petition case, the procedure stipulated, should be decided upon within a month if at all possible; for the more complex cases, an extension of one more month was permissible, but the petitioners should be informed of the reasons.[56]

As part of the effort to create "an honest and efficient government," Chiang Ching-kuo also acted more decisively against corruption. Beginning in the summer of 1972, more and more cases of corruption were brought into the open and the culprits severely punished. In August 1972, in connection with the prosecution of a smuggling case, a number of fairly high-ranking officers of the Taiwan

Garrison Command were publicly arrested and convicted, marking the first time in many years that officers of the feared and powerful security unit had been subject to laws.[57] In early 1973, Wang Cheng-yi, chief of the Personnel Administration Bureau of the Executive Yuan was prosecuted for accepting bribery in connection with building housing projects for government civil servants. He was

1. Be thrifty, not extravagant.
2. Pay taxes and do not manipulate tax loopholes.
3. Obey traffic regulations and maintain public order.
4. Obey the laws and do not bribe.
5. Invest in production, not in speculation.
6. Merchants, do not hoard goods and drive up prices.
7. Individuals and households, help one another.
8. Prevent juvenile delinquency.[59]

From the perspective of Chiang Ching-kuo and the government, the program was a logical move: administrative reforms, to be successful, must be supplemented by social reforms, with society taking part in the efforts. The stress was placed on being thrifty and contributing to the common good. The government realized that if Taiwan were to move on with industrialization and economic development, the need for capital would be great indeed. Furthermore, conspicuous consumption by the wealthier classes was judged as corrupting public morality. However, this social program was difficult to enforce since for many years the rich in Taiwan, particularly the entrepreneur class in Taipei, had acquired a highly extravagant life style, whose habits were not easy to change. Nevertheless, by the summer of 1973, due to the effects of the world economy and the energy crisis, the government had become very preoccupied with economic stability. The injunctions to be thrifty, to pay taxes, and not to hoard goods and drive up prices necessarily acquired a sense of urgency.

Beyond administrative and social reforms, Chiang Ching-kuo was particularly concerned with youth affairs; consequently, measures were adopted to tackle youth problems. This concern of his, parenthetically, was not something new; his involvement with youth groups was well-known. The China Youth Corps set up in 1952 under his leadership had, through the years, engaged in a wide range of activities, the goal of which was defined as "to help the young people in their intellectual and physical development and to mobilize and train them for national reconstruction."[60] More precisely, the Youth Corps was a kind of hybrid between summer camps in Western countries and youth organizations in the Communist blocks. No doubt, the Corps had served as a power base for Chiang Ching-kuo since the fifties. Many of his close associates from his Kiangsi days were appointed to important positions at the Corps. For more than two decades, Chiang Ching-kuo was presented by his supporters as a teacher and great leader of youth.

In the summer of 1971, during the time of ferment for political reforms, the Youth Corps for the first time in two decades sponsored a Conference on National Construction.[61] It was designed in part to accommodate the young people's desire for participation in affairs of state, with students from different universities and colleges given an opportunity to exchange views with governmental officials. A number of ministries, including the Ministry of Foreign Affairs and the Ministry of Education, and five universities took part in the conference. Student participants were selected by the different university administrations, with each university assigned a quota. Altogether, 1,219 students were chosen. The bulk of the students were either graduate students, juniors, or seniors; the average age was twenty-two. After the group was divided into sections according to their interests, they heard reports from government officials and participated in discussions in group settings. An innovative aspect of the conference was that they were given the opportunity to visit the Bureau of Investigation of the Ministry of Justice and the Taiwan Garrison Command and to question officials of these two departments.[62] To the degree that these government organs had been dreaded and feared, their access to the students unmistakably provoked a great deal of interest.

On the whole the conference was successful. The most serious criticism, it appears, was that "the government officials tended not to speak the truth, but approached their assignments as a kind of ritual performance; they did not honestly describe and analyze the policy measures adopted by the government." A high percentage of the participants interviewed, moreover, suggested that they had hoped to have more opportunity to express their opinions. As to the perceived influences of their opinions on government policy, the student participants were not highly optimistic, though a sub-

Prior to and immediately following his assumption of the premiership, Chiang Ching-kuo made a serious effort to reach youth. On Youth Day 1972, he called on youth to contribute their wisdom, courage, and strength to complete the historic mission of defeating the Communists and to reconstruct the nation.[65] Some six months later, he spoke to university graduates in military training and again urged them to sacrifice for the nation and shoulder their historic missions.[66] In November 1972, in the ceremony of presenting citations to the ten most outstanding youths of the year, he once more called on youth to work hard, not only for themselves but also for the nation.[67] By the summer of 1973, the government began to adopt concrete policy measures on youth affairs. In May 1973, a Youth Work Conference was sponsored by the Ministry of Education, presided over by Minister Chiang Yen-shih. Participants on the government side included Chiang Ching-kuo; Mr. Pan Chen-chew, director of the Commission for Youth Assistance and Guidance; Mr. Frederick Chien; Mr. Lee Huan, deputy director of the Youth Corps; Mr. Wang Wei-lung; and many other high-ranking government officials. As representatives of the youth, some fifty young men and women also participated. In this conference Chiang Ching-kuo reiterated his view that the government was committed to helping youth in creating a bright future. "The government regards youth," he said, "as the new force for the nation; only when the youth and the government are fully integrated and become one body, will the nation have hope and the youth have future."[68] As a result of this conference, the Guideline for Youth Work was adopted.

Among other things, the guideline committed the government to aid youth in understanding the affairs of state through such channels as the Conference on National Construction and the Forum on the State of the Nation, in providing jobs for youth, in assisting youth in starting enterprises, and in helping youth in pursuing higher studies. [69]

Three months later Chiang Ching-kuo called in Mr. Chiang Yen-shih, Mr. Lee Huan, Mr. Pan Chen-chew, and other government officials involved with youth work and reviewed with them the implementation of the guideline. He pointed out that youth work was a long-term project, requiring planning and coordination. He urged that, for the present time, emphasis be placed on helping graduates of junior and senior high schools who had not gone on with their studies, university and college graduates without jobs, as well as on the training and welfare of youth engaged in agricultural work and industry. [70]

Through the Commission for Youth Assistance and Guidance, plans were made for aiding youth in settling in rural areas. In particular youth with training in agricultural science and technique were encouraged to live and work in rural areas, while youth from the countryside living in the cities were induced to return to their native places, with such persons being given preferable treatment in terms of loans, land, agricultural tools, seeds, fertilizer, etc., so that they could engage in agricultural enterprises. [71] A model agricultural community was also scheduled to be set up in the northern part of Taiwan, to include agriculture, animal husbandry, vegetable cultivation, and fishery. Recreational and residential units were also planned for the community. The project was anticipated to be completed in 1976, and upon its completion, to be leased or sold by units to young entrepreneurs. The participating young entrepreneurs would be organized into some kind of cooperatives, the plan envisaged, so that they could achieve greater efficiency in production. It was also anticipated that they would have the opportunity of receiving professional training abroad to further improve their expertise. [72]

More and more measures to help youth seek jobs were given priority by the government, and following the decision at the end of 1973 to go all out toward achieving the status of a developed nation, these measures were tied closely with manpower needs and economic development. [73]

Another reform measure put into effect by Chiang Ching-kuo and his administration was agricultural modernization. Realizing that the peasants had not shared equitably in the economic development, the government moved to accelerate agricultural development, and by doing so, aimed at improving the living standard of the peasants. In a Conference on Agricultural Construction in September

[several lines illegible/faded]

the market price as the criterion. If and when the market price fell far too low, the government promised to purchase rice at a reasonable price.

2. The land surtax levied in support of the free nine-year educational system was abolished, so as to reduce the burden on the peasants.

3. The terms of agricultural loans would be relaxed.

4. The agricultural marketing system would be reformed.

5. Investment in the infrastructure of the countryside would be increased, including irrigation projects and facilities for public health.

6. The use of integrated techniques of production would be speeded up.

7. Specified agricultural production zones would be set up.

8. Agricultural research and extension services would be strengthened.

9. Factories in rural areas would be encouraged to use rural labor and increase the income of the peasants.[74]

For these nine projects, the government decided to allocate two billion new Taiwan dollars through a supplementary budget, and it was anticipated that they should be put into effect not later than the beginning of 1973. In his speech at the conference, Chiang Ching-kuo urged the peasants to take the initiative and participate in the new agricultural construction movement. Comparing it to the Land Reform Movement in the early fifties, he predicted success.[75]

Following the instructions of Chiang Ching-kuo, the different ministries and government units related to agricultural development began to set up task forces to implement the projects. A request for a supplementary budget of NT$2 billion was made to the Legislative Yuan. As the Minister of Economic Affairs Sun Yun-suan made clear, the bulk of the money would go for building irrigation projects and roads and improving public health facilities in the countryside. Also, the government was determined to encourage setting up factories in rural areas so that rural manpower could be efficiently used.[76] In his report to the Legislative Yuan in March 1973, Chiang Ching-kuo again reiterated that the program's goal was to improve the peasants' living standard. However, he did not anticipate that a great deal would be accomplished within the span of a year or two; rather, if necessary, supplementary budgets would be requested again in the years to come. He particularly emphasized that, in the long range, the goal was nothing less than the modernization of agriculture.[77]

As expected, the Legislative Yuan approved the budget request in April 1973.[78] By August 1973, the Agricultural Development Act was enacted, making modernization of agriculture government policy. It was anticipated that within a decade the bulk of the agricultural sector's problems would be solved, and that the inequalities between the agricultural and nonagricultural sectors would be substantially eliminated.[79]

This ambitious plan to modernize agriculture was well received by society. Newspapers hailed it as an historic decision.[80] Commenting on the nine-point project, Ta-hsueh tsa-chih praised Chiang Ching-kuo for having kept his promise to serve the people and for having given the peasants their due. However, it suggested that to solve the problems in the agricultural sector, stress on development was not sufficient; rather, the government should help pay the debts incurred by peasants in the past decades. Furthermore, the

journal continued, since any good policy risks failure in its implementation, if the government did not rid itself of corrupt officials,
corruption and incompetence must be dealt with seriously so that
the program could prove successful.[81] Nevertheless, such massive
commitment of resources should prove beneficial to the agricultural
sector; and given the government's determination, more funds could

Given the urge to promote industrialization and international trade
on which the survival of Taiwan depended, he did not find it possible
to move boldly on the issue of the workers' welfare. It was not
until spring of 1973 that the government began to turn to the workers' problems. In a conference at the Ministry of the Interior on
industrial safety and health measures, the participants agreed that,
among other things, a Labor Safety and Health Act should be enacted
as soon as possible, that inspection should be strengthened, and that
both the employers and the labor force should be urged to take safety and health seriously.[82]

In late April the government announced the adoption of three
measures for the improvement of the workers' living standard: to
promote a comprehensive program of vocational training and to en-
sure job security; to strengthen labor safety and health care; and,
within the framework of "guaranteeing stability of production," to
improve laboring conditions such as readjustment of basic wages,
rationalization of working hours, implementation of leave with pay,
as well as development and consolidation of labor unions, etc.[83]

In May, the Executive Yuan adopted the Protection of Workers'
Interests and Improvement of their Living Standard Program. It
listed seven measures for immediate implementation and nine for
further study and investigation.[84] The former included such items
as safety and health measures for workers, eight-hour shifts for
adult workers in principle, and eight-hour shifts for minor workers
aged 14 to 16 without exception, etc. The latter referred to mea-

sures dealing with a basic wage and required new laws or the revision of existing laws.[85] A month later, the Labor Safety Act was adopted by the Executive Yuan and submitted to the Legislative Yuan for enactment.[86] Discussion of the Labor Union Act was held, the revision of which had been completed in 1972.[87] Also the Ministry of the Interior convened a meeting to discuss improvement of labor insurance and decided to initiate a comprehensive investigation of both privately and publicly owned enterprises, factories, and companies employing more than ten persons and to severely punish any which were discovered to have violated the insurance regulations.[88]

A year later the Ministry of the Interior, the Ministry of Economic Affairs, and the Directorate General of Budget, Accounting and Statistics were said to have completed a study of the readjustment of the basic wage and would move towards implementation at a suitable time.[89] However, the Minister of the Interior pointed out that the Labor Union Act was still in the process of discussion and that employment insurance, given the complexity of the issues involved, could not be taken up for some time.[90]

This series of measures for protecting and promoting the workers' welfare, both adopted and promised, was modest indeed. But if the measures were implemented and enforced vigorously, some improvement in the workers' living standard and working conditions presumably would be gained. However, beginning in 1973, given the economic difficulties derived from the worldwide energy crisis and the decision of Chiang Ching-kuo to go all out for basic economic projects so that Taiwan could achieve the status of a developed nation, it appeared that the workers' welfare would not have priority for some years to come. The developed nation concept preempted all other priorities.

To sum up, the ruling party and government, particularly after the assumption of power by Chiang Ching-kuo, adopted over the span of two years a series of reform measures. In part, they were the results of the intellectual ferment; in part they reflected Chiang Ching-kuo's keen instinct for power consolidation and long-held convictions. Primarily, these measures were directed towards broadening the popular base of the people's representative bodies at the national level, recruiting young men of talent, effecting administrative and social reforms, and improving the welfare of youth, peasants, and workers. On the whole, they fell short of what the intellectuals had strived for. However, they did achieve some tangible results; and if continued vigorously, they offered great potential. Moreover, by adopting these reform measures, Chiang Ching-kuo had consolidated his power and position, making it more difficult for any group to challenge his authority in the near future.

V. CONCLUSION

The intellectual ferment for political reforms in Taiwan between 1971 and 1973 was a dramatic episode in the political annals
of the Republic of China.   It drew upon a long and honored tradition
[several lines illegible/faded]
were prepared to act, to take risks, and to make sacrifices.   For
a while they were optimistic that they were working with the tide of
history.   Yet they were destined to be frustrated; and many of them
were made to suffer for their commitment to political change.

To account for the intellectuals' failure to achieve their goals,
a few points may be made.   To begin with, the young intellectuals
still operated in a traditional manner even though they were severely
critical of tradition.   They presented themselves as the conscience
of the people, spoke to the ills of society, and took to the streets
to agitate for change.   Yet beyond a certain point, they did not go.
Through the two-year span, they did not at any time move to form
an opposition party, though they referred time and again to the need
for precisely such a countervailing force.   Of course, it was possible that had they moved to organize an opposition party, they
would have been put down by force by the ruling party if it felt
that should have been necessary.   Nevertheless, it could be argued
that if the university professors and students had announced the formation of a new political party at the height of the ferment, e.g.,
November or December 1971, they might have created a new situation with intriguing possibilities.   They might not have succeeded,
but the ruling party would have faced a much more serious challenge.   Since they did not choose such a course of action, the initiative ultimately passed from their hands to the party and government, particularly with the assumption of power by Chiang Ching-
kuo in the summer of 1972.

Equally crucial was the fact that the intellectuals did not vigorously seek the support of diverse segments of the society. The young university professors and students pleaded time and again on behalf of the peasants, the workers, and the poor; yet no attempt was made to draw them into the ferment for change. The "social service corps," as indicated earlier, was a field study rather than a mobilization effort to link up with the citizens. Granted, if the intellectuals had reached out vigorously for support, they might have provoked severe reprisals from the party and government; yet not to do so definitely isolated them. As a result, only a few young men of the entrepreneur class, such as Chang Shao-wen, a coauthor of An Analysis of the Social Forces in Taiwan and secretary general of China Branch, International Junior Chamber of Commerce, supported the ferment for political reforms. As for the peasants and workers, though they were desperately in need of reforms, their potential for effecting change was left unexplored. A few letters from workers to the Ta-hsueh tsa-chih merely testified to their presence as well as their impotence.

Furthermore, the intellectual group was divided and did not act as a coherent body when the ruling party and government exerted pressures on them. As had been indicated above, the core group of the Ta-hsueh tsa-chih broke up almost as soon as they began to confront the government. The activities of Professor Hungdah Chiu and his friends definitely weakened the journal's position. Again, when Professor Chen Ku-ying was attacked in April 1972, university professors and students on the whole rallied to his defense; yet when he and Professor Wang Shao-po and their students were detained by the authorities a year later, hardly any intellectual publicly came to their defense. This reflected at least in part the genuine disagreements between Professor Chen Ku-ying and Wang Shao-po and their colleagues. Likewise, in the case of Mr. Chang Ching-hang's campaign for a seat in the City Council of Taipei and his entanglement with the party, many of his friends in academics and on the journal criticized him for using the journal for his personal short-term political gain, thus creating a division within the intellectual community.

Finally, the response from the ruling party and government substantially deflected the pressures for reforms. By skillful use of concessions, rewards, and coercion, the ruling elite exploited the weaknesses and inexperience of the young intellectuals.

Obviously, the ruling party and government pursued a two-part policy. On the one hand, Chiang Ching-kuo accommodated young university professors and students by recruiting some young men and women of academic background into the decision-making echelon, while at the same time he moved against those who were judged a threat to the authorities. Professors Chen Ku-ying and

[illegible]

dated his power.

The intellectual ferment for political reforms subsided as abruptly as it began. As has been shown, the Tiao-yu-tai Movement for all practical purposes had exhausted itself by the summer of 1972 and the ferment for political reforms became dormant in the summer of 1973. Subsequently, young university professors and students again found themselves under severe pressures.

For the near future, provided the status of Taiwan as a de facto autonomous political entity is not threatened, Chiang Ching-kuo's power is unchallengeable. The reform measures he has adopted so far could lead to substantial political and social change in Taiwan if he is determined to implement them vigorously. The trend is clear that the thrust of the reform effort is to assure the survival of Taiwan through economic development and international trade. Consequently, it can be predicted that the entrepreneur class will continue to receive favors and the technocrats will acquire more power in the administration. The welfare of the peasants and workers, particularly the latter, will have to wait for some time to come. As for the young intellectuals committed to liberalism, genuine political structural reforms, and the emergence of an opposition party, they are faced with a long and lonely road.

Nevertheless, the intellectual ferment for political reforms in Taiwan between 1971 and 1973 indicated that a young generation had come of age and that it had acquired some political experience. In the years to come they are bound to agitate for change again, for their basic aspirations have not been and are not likely to be satisfied by the ruling elite. But as to when they might again move into the political stage, what course of action they might pursue, and how successful they might be, only the future can tell. However, a scenario suggests itself, given the rather poor health of Chiang Ching-kuo and the power concentrated in his person. His death or incapacity to govern could create a power vacuum. At that time, if the autonomy of Taiwan is not imminently threatened by mainland China, the young intellectuals could possibly regroup and, drawing upon their experience in the early 1970s, move to organize an opposition party in their effort to create an open and democratic society on Taiwan.

Chapter I

1. The Wen-hsing [Literary star] group referred to a loosely

ment and other crimes, was arrested by the authorities in 1971.

The Szu-yu-yen she [Thought and word association] which publishes the Szu-yu-yen [Thought and word] was organized in the
early sixties.   Primarily composed of young university professors and researchers at the Academia Sinica, it was dedicated
to the assimilation of new knowledge and discussion of "urgent
issues" facing the nation.   However, when faced with harassment from the ruling party and the government, the group
avoided any political involvement and concentrated its effort
in making the journal a prestigious journal in the humanities
and social sciences.   When Chiang Ching-kuo assumed government power in May 1972, a number of the association's members were recruited into government service and given fairly
high posts.

The Ta-hsueh tsa-chih she [The intellectual journal association]
which publishes the Ta-hsueh tsa-chih [The intellectual] was
formed in 1968.   It was at that time primarily a group of
young Taiwanese intellectuals.   For its first three years the
journal emphasized the role and responsibility of the intellectual in a changing society.   After 1971 it took a leadership
role in agitating for political reforms.   More will be said
about the journal in this study.

2. For the Taiwanese Independence Movement, see Douglass Mendal, The Politics of Formosan Nationalism (Berkeley, Univer-

Chapter I Notes

sity of California Press, 1970). This work is highly critical
of the Nationalist rule of Taiwan. Ironically, for the past few
years and particularly since the China-United States rapprochement in 1971, many Taiwanese Independence Movement leaders
have returned to cooperate with the Nationalist Party. Apparently they have judged the Nationalist rule preferable to
Chinese Communist absorption of Taiwan. For this trend,
see Melvin Gurtov, "Recent Developments on Formosa," The
China Quarterly, no. 31 (July-September 1967); also J. Bruce
Jacobs, "Taiwan 1972: Political Season," Asian Survey, vol.
13, no. 1, January 1973.

3. For the early years of the Nationalist rule of Taiwan, see
Fred W. Riggs, Formosa Under the Chinese Nationalist Rule,
1952 by the American Institute of Pacific Relations, Inc. Re-
printed 1972 by Octagon Books. Also consult Neil H. Jacoby,
U.S. Aid to Taiwan (New York: Fred A. Praeger, 1966).
For a more critical view of the Nationalist rule in Taiwan,
see George H. Kerr, Formosa Betrayed (Boston: Houghton-
Mifflin, 1965); Douglass Mendal, The Politics of Formosan
Nationalism. For a general survey of different aspects of
life in Taiwan, see Mark Mancall, ed., Formosa Today (New
York: Praeger, 1964).

4. For the Lei Chen case, see Douglass Mendal, The Politics of
Formosan Nationalism, pp. 114-117. For a collection of documents with comments on the case, see Shih Ping-chih, ed., "Col-
lections of Documents on the Lei Chen Case" (in Chinese),
4 parts, in Jen-wu yu ssu-hsiang [Men and ideas], no. 42-45,
September-December 1970, Hong Kong

5. See Hai-wai lun-t'an [World forum], November 1, 1960, New
York City.

6. For the case of Professor Yin Hai-kwong, see "In Memory of
Mr. Yin Hai-kwong" (in Chinese), Jen-wu, no. 31, October 15,
1969, p. 4; "Important Events in the Last Three Years of Mr.
Yin Hai-kwong's Life" (in Chinese), Jen-wu, no. 31, p. 5 and
p. 32. Also Yin Hai-kwong, "How I Was Forced to Leave the
National Taiwan University" (in Chinese), Jen-wu, no. 31,
pp. 8-13.

Chapter I Notes

7. New York Times, July 3, July 7, 1969. Also see Sun Kuang-
    han, "A Man's [Po Yang's] Fate" (in Chinese), Jen-wu, no. 55,
    October 1971 and no. 56, November 1971. Sun Kuang-han,
    "Mr. Chiang Ching-kuo, I Beg You to Release Mr. Po Yang

9. See Chou Chin-ming, ed., The Institute of Pacific Relations
    and the John K. Fairbank Clique (in Chinese), 3 volumes,
    in particular the third volume (Taipei, Taiwan, 1968-1969).
    For a critical review of this work see, among others, Leonard
    H. D. Fordon and Sidney Chang, "John K. Fairbank and His
    Critics in the Republic of China," Journal of Asian Studies,
    vol. 30, no. 1, November 1970.

10. See Chen Ku-ying, for his reference to the attack and harass-
    ment of the Szu-yu-yen group by the government in "Let Stu-
    dent Movement Develop" (in Chinese), Ta-hsueh, no. 49,
    January 20, 1972, p. 64.

11. See Chow Tse-tsung, The May Fourth Movement (Stanford
    University Press, 1960).

12. See Neil H. Jacoby, U.S. Aid to Taiwan; Mark Mancall,
    Formosa Today; also Hungdah Chiu, ed., China and the
    Question of Taiwan: Documents and Analysis (New York:
    Praeger, 1973).

13. See Chang Ching-hang, et al., An Analysis of the Social
    Forces in Taiwan (in Chinese) (Taipei: The Universal
    Press, 1971). This book was originally published as a
    series of articles in Ta-hsueh tsa-chih beginning in July
    1971.

110

Chapter I Notes

14. See Chow Tao-chi, "On Rejuvenation of the People's Representatives at the National Level" (in Chinese), Tung-fang tsa-chih
[Eastern miscellany], May 1971, Taipei. Cited in Chen Shao-
ting, "On the Problems of Reelection of the People's Representatives at the National Level" (in Chinese), Ta-hsueh, no. 46,
October 1971, p. 16.

15. See note 14 above.

16. Chung-yang jih-pao, international edition, December 21, 1969.

17. J. Bruce Jacobs, "Recent Leadership and Political Trends in
Taiwan," China Quarterly, no. 45, January-March 1971, p. 135.

18. For a more comprehensive study of the Tiao-yu-tai affairs,
consult Hungdah Chiu, "A Study of the Tiao-yu-tai Islets Problem" (in Chinese), Chengchi Law Review, vol. 16, June 1972.
Hungdah Chiu, ed., "A Chronicle of Important Events Relating
to the Tiao-yu-tai Islets" (in Chinese), Ta-hsueh, no. 40,
April 1971, pp. 19-24. Also Research Institute on National
Affairs, Special Issue on Tiao-yu-tai Incident (in Chinese),
New York, 1971. The account in the following paragraph
is taken primarily from these sources.

19. Chung-yang jih-pao, March 6, 1971.

20. Hungdah Chiu, "A Chronicle of Important Events."

21. For an account of an active participant of the movement in the
United States, see Lee Teh-yu, "My Participation and Reflections on the Protect Tiao-yu-tai Movement" (in Chinese), Ta-
hsueh, no. 49, January 1972, pp. 69-70. Also see Hsing
Chien, "The Patriotic Movement of the Chinese Students in
the U.S." (in Chinese), Hwa-mei jih-pao, New York, February 2, 1971. Reprinted in Ta-hsueh, no. 40, April 1971,
p. 25.

22. See Chung-wu Kung, "A New May Fourth Movement?" Bulletin
of Concerned Asian Scholars, double issue, Summer-Fall 1971,
vol. 3, no. 3 and vol. 3, no. 4, San Francisco, California,
pp. 61-72.

Chapter I Notes

23. Chung-yang jih-pao, March 19, 1971.

24. Chung-yang jih-pao, February 5, 1971.

25. [illegible] "Prevent the Contamination of Over-
[illegible]

26. [illegible]

27. [illegible]
National Taiwan University (in Chinese), Ta-hsueh, no. 41,
May 1971, pp. 6-9.

28. See "Our View on the Tiao-yu-tai Issue," Ta-hsueh, no. 40,
April 1971, p. 17.

29. Feng Hou-ping, "Protect the Tiao-yu-tai Islands." Also Lee
Chung-min, "Students at National Normal University Defend
the Tiao-yu-tai Islands" (in Chinese), Ta-hsueh, no. 41,
May 1971, pp. 10-13; Wu Chin-en, "An Account of the Protect Tiao-yu-tai Islands Movement at National Chengchi University" (in Chinese), Ta-hsueh, no. 41, pp. 14-16. The account
in the following paragraphs is taken from these sources.

30. See Mou Han, "An Account of the June 17th Student Demonstra-
tion" (in Chinese), Ta-hsueh, no. 43, July 1971, pp. 24-27.
Also Tai-ta ching-lien [Taiwan university youth], "A Few
Words on Behalf of Protect Tiao-yu-tai Movement" (in Chinese),
June 1971.

31. "A Statement Severely Warning the Governments of U.S. and
Japan Against Aggression on Tiao-yu-tai Islands" (in Chinese),
editorial, Ta-hsueh, no. 43, July 1971, pp. 2-3.

32. New York Times, July 16, 1971.

33. New York Times, July 17, 1971. Also see Chung-yang jih-
pao, international edition, July 17, 1971.

Chapter I Notes

34. New York Times, July 16, 1971.

35. See Chiang Kai-shek, "The Stand of Our Nation and the Spirit of Our People," a speech delivered to the National Security Council on June 15, 1971, trans. in Free China Weekly, July 30, 1970.

36. From this author's notes.

37. From this author's notes.

38. Huang Chu-kwei, "Our Nation's Situation After the Nixon-Chou Communique" (in Chinese), Ta-hsueh, no. 51-52, April 1972, pp. 14-17.

39. New York Times, October 26, 1971. Also see Chung-yang jih-pao, international edition, October 27, 1971.

40. Chung-yang jih-pao, international edition, October 27, 1971.

41. From this author's notes.

42. See Chang Ching-hang, et al., "In Commemoration of the Sixth Anniversary of the Republic of China; A Word of Expostulation on the State of the Nation" (in Chinese), Ta-hsueh, no. 46, October 1971, pp. 1-10. The demands of political reforms are taken up in Chapter II.

43. From this author's notes.

44. Chung-yang jih-pao, international edition, February 21, 1972.

45. Chung-yang jih-pao, international edition, February 22, 1972. See also New York Times, February 22, 1972.

46. Chung-yang jih-pao, international edition, February 29, 1972. See also New York Times, February 29, 1972.

47. Chung-yang jih-pao, international edition, May 10, 1972.

48. See "Interview with Chang Tai-hsiang" (in Chinese), the president of the Protect Tiao-yu-tai Movement at National Taiwan University, in Fa Yen, April 17, 1972.

Chapter I Notes

49. From this author's notes.

50. For Professor Kao Chun's statement and diverse opinions on
    ~~this issue, see the verbatim report of "The Forum on the~~
    [illegible]

[illegible]

[illegible]

~~52.~~ the Chinese Communist Bandits" (in Chinese), editorial, Chung-
    yang jih-pao, September 3, 1972.

53. Chung-yang jih-pao, international edition, September 12, 1972.

54. Ibid.

55. New York Times, August 17, 1972.

56. Chung-yang jih-pao, international edition, September 19, 1972.

57. J. Bruce Jacobs, "Taiwan 1972: Political Season," Asian
    Survey, January 1973, p. 103.

58. Chung-yang jih-pao, international edition, September 22, 1972.

59. Chung-yang jih-pao, international edition, September 30, 1972.

60. New York Times, October 1, 1972.

61. Ibid.

62. New York Times, October 2, 1972.

63. See a collection of articles on nationalism by students of Na-
    tional Taiwan University in Yang Yung-i, ed., The Debate on
    Nationalism at the National Taiwan University (in Chinese)

Chapter I Notes

(Taipei: Hsin-sheng Publishers, May 1973). Also see Pai Li-an, "Intellectual Youth in Taiwan Debate Nationalism" (in Chinese), The United Quarterly, vol. 5, no. 2, July 1973, New York, New York, pp. 5-13.

64. This statement by Professor Chen Ku-ying is taken from Pai Li-an, "Intellectual Youth in Taiwan, " p. 10.

65. For example, see Hu Chu-min, "Reflections on the Forum on Nationalism: The Views of a Student at National Taiwan University" (in Chinese), in Yang Yung-i, ed., The Debate on Nationalism, pp. 10-14.

66. For example, see Huang Tao-lin, "Reflections on the Forum on Nationalism: The Views of a Chinese" (in Chinese), in Yang Yung-i, ed., The Debate on Nationalism, pp. 20-25.

Chapter II Notes

1. For example, see the interview with Professor Wang Shao-po in Fa Yen, April 17, 1972. Also see Chung-wu Kung, "A New May Fourth Movement," for a similar view on the Protect Tiao-yu-tai Movement in the United States.

2. Lu Fu-chen, et al., "A Letter to Mr. Chiang Ching-kuo " (in Chinese), Ta-hsueh, no. 37, January 1971, p. 17.

3. Chen Ku-ying, "On Toleration and Understanding" (in Chinese), Ta-hsueh, no. 37, pp. 6-7.

4. Chen Shao-ting, "Academic Freedom and National Security" (in Chinese), Ta-hsueh, no. 37, pp. 11-12.

5. Chang Ching-hang, "Remove Three Barriers of Modernization" (in Chinese), Ta-hsueh, no. 37, pp. 8-10.

6. Shao Hsiang-feng, "The Problem of Economic Development of Taiwan" (in Chinese), Ta-hsueh, no. 37, pp. 4-5.

7. Chang Ching-hang, et al., "Commemoration of the Sixtieth Anniversary of the Republic of China: A Word of Expostula-

Chapter II Notes

tion on the State of the Nation" (in Chinese), Ta-hsueh, no. 46, October 1971, pp. 1-10.

8. Ibid., p. 1.

[illegible faded lines]

13. Ibid., p. 6.

14. Ibid., p. 7.

15. Ibid., pp. 8-9.

16. Ibid., p. 10.

17. See Chen Shao-ting, "On the Problem of Reelection of the People's Representatives at the National Level: With Comments on Mr. Chou Tao-chi's Proposals" (in Chinese), Ta-hsueh, no. 46, October 1971, pp. 13-16.

18. Lin Chen-hung, "I Urge the Government to Consider an Amnesty for Political Prisoners" (in Chinese), Ta-hsueh, no. 46, October 1971, pp. 20-21.

19. Chung-yang jih-pao, international edition, October 29, 1971.

20. Liu Fu-sheng, "The Story of Wang Hsing-ching" (in Chinese), Lien-ho jih-pao, November 19, 1971.

21. Wang Hsing-ching, et al., "The Time of Reawakening Is Here" (in Chinese), Ta-hsueh, no. 47, November 1971, p. 23.

22. See the collection of newspaper articles in "The Reactions of the Society to Mr. Wang Hsing-ching's Reawakening" (in Chinese), Ta-hsueh, no. 48, December 1971, pp. 59-62.

Chapter II Notes

23. Ho Wen-cheng, "An Invitation to the Intellectuals" (in Chinese), Ta-hsueh, no. 47, November 1971, p. 25.

24. Chung-yang jih-pao, international edition, December 27, 1971.

25. For the background of Professor Chang Ya-yung and his role in the drafting of the declaration, see Chang Ya-yung, "On Student Movement" (in Chinese), Ta-hsueh, no. 53, May 1972, pp. 37-46.

26. Chung-yang jih-pao, international edition, December 27, 1971.

27. See "After the Withdrawal and Expulsion from the United Nations" (in Chinese), Chung-hwa tsa-chih, no. 100, November 1971, pp. 4-11. Also Fang Chun-ta, et al., "On a Word of Expostulation" (in Chinese), Chung-hwa tsa-chih, no. 100, November 1971, pp. 49-50. This latter article is an exchange between readers and the editor of the Chung-hwa tsa-chih.

28. Wang Wen-hsin, et al., "Nine Treatises on the Affairs of the Nation" (in Chinese), Ta-hsueh, no. 49, January 1972, pp. 7-44.

29. Professor Hu Fu and this writer participated in the discussion and drafting of the treatise on fundamental human rights for which Professor Chen Ku-ying served as rapporteur.

30. See Wang Wen-hsin, et al., "Nine Treatises," pp. 21-24.

31. Ibid., pp. 25-28.

32. Hu Fu, "Eliminate the Obstacles of Political Reforms" (in Chinese), Lien-ho jih-pao, March 7, 1972.

33. Hu Fu, "Establish the Political Concept of Reason" (in Chinese), Lien-ho jih-pao, January 4, 1973.

34. Wen Chun-i, "Reform and Anti-Reform" (in Chinese), Lien-ho jih-pao, October 12, 1972.

35. Yuan Sung-hsi, "Democracy, Science and Education" (in Chinese), Lien-ho jih-pao, October 10, 1972. Also see Yuan

Chapter II Notes

Sung-hsi, "Political Reform and Social Reform," Ta-hsueh, no. 66, July 1973, pp. 4-5, in which he discusses the problems of building a new state from the old society.

the Present Time" (in Chinese), Ta-hsueh, no. 46, October 1971, pp. 32-34. Also see Feng Hou-ping, "On the Review System of Student Publications" (in Chinese), Ta-hsueh, no. 46, October 1971, pp. 59-60.

39. See the verbatim account of the forum on "Freedom of Speech at National Taiwan University" (in Chinese), part 1, Ta-hsueh, no. 47, November 1971, p. 26.

40. Ibid., p. 27.

41. Ibid., pp. 27-28.

42. Ibid., p. 32.

43. Ibid., pp. 29-33.

44. "Freedom of Speech" (in Chinese), part 2, Ta-hsueh, no. 48, December 1971, p. 44.

45. Ibid., pp. 46-50.

46. Ibid., p. 46.

47. The verbatim account of this forum has not been published, with the exception of Professor Chen Ku-ying's speech which was published in Ta-hsueh, no. 49, January 1972, as "Let Student Movement Develop!" pp. 64-68. The account of the following paragraphs is taken from this author's notes.

Chapter II Notes

48. Chen Ku-ying, "Let the Student Movement Develop!" p. 67.

49. Ibid.

50. Lien-ho jih-pao, December 8, 1971.

51. Wang Hu-su, "The Origins of the Social Service Corps of National Taiwan University" (in Chinese), Ta-hsueh, no. 49, January 1972, pp. 62-63. See also Chen Li-hsiang, et al., "An Objective Evaluation of the Social Service Corps of National Taiwan University" (in Chinese), Ta-hsueh, no. 55, July 1972, pp. 25-31. The account in the following paragraphs is taken from this source.

52. See Chung-yang jih-pao, international edition, May 18, 1972.

53. See Wang Wen-hsin, et al., "Nine Treatises," pp. 11-14.

54. See Lee Ching-yun, "On Recruitment of Men of Talent: An Interview with Professor Hu Fu" (in Chinese), Chung-kuo shih-pao, [China times], May 31, 1972.

55. Lin Pu-pai, "On the Recruitment of Men of Talent and the System of Testimony" (in Chinese), Ta-hsueh, no. 54, June 1972, p. 11.

56. Yin Tsou, "From Where Come Men of Talent?" (in Chinese), Ta-hsueh, no. 51-52, combined issue, April 1972, pp. 20-21.

57. Mab Huang, "On the Recruitment of Men of Talent" (in Chinese), Ta-hsueh, no. 54, June 1972, p. 12.

58. See Chow Tao-chi, "On Our Parliament at the Present Time" (in Chinese), Tung-fang tsa-chih [Eastern miscellany], June 1969. Also for his reiteration on this point in his debate with Mr. Chen Shao-ting, see the verbatim account of "Debate on the Complete Reelection of the People's Representatives at the National Level," Ta-hsueh, no. 49, January 1972, p. 81.

59. See Professor Chow Tao-chi's statement in his debate with Mr. Chen Shao-ting, in the verbatim account of "Debate on the Complete Reelection of the People's Representatives," p. 81.

Chapter II Notes

60. <u>Ibid.</u>, p. 82. This series of proposals was first set out in Chow Tao-chi, "The Problems of Rejuvenation of People's Representatives at the National Level" (in Chinese), <u>Tung-fang tsa-chih</u>, May 1971, and further revised in his article in <u>Tien</u>

[illegible faded text]

63. <u>Ibid.</u>, p. 15.

64. See the comments of the editor preceding the verbatim account of "Debate on the Complete Reelection of the People's Representatives," p. 80.

65. <u>Ibid.</u>

66. See the verbatim account of "Debate on the Complete Reelection of the People's Representatives," p. 82.

67. <u>Ibid.</u>, p. 83.

68. Chen Shao-ting, "Further Thought on the Problem of Reelection of the People's Representatives at the National Level," <u>Ta-hsueh</u>, no. 49, January 1972, p. 93.

69. <u>Ibid.</u>, p. 97.

70. See "The Voice of the Youth in Support of Complete Reelection of the People's Representatives at the National Level" (in Chinese), <u>Ta-hsueh</u>, no. 49, January 1972, p. 90. Also Hung Shan-hsiang, "My Opinion in Support of the Complete Reelection of the People's Representatives at the National Level (in Chinese), <u>Ta-hsueh</u>, no. 49, January 1972, pp. 91-92.

71. Cited in Chen Shao-ting, "Further Thought on the Problem," p. 97.

Chapter II Notes

72. Hung Shan-hsiang, "My Opinion in Support," p. 91.

73. Chang Ching-hang, et al., An Analysis of the Social Forces in Taiwan. The following paragraph is taken from this book.

74. Ibid., p. 49.

75. Ibid., p. 50.

76. Ibid., pp. 51-52.

77. Chen Ku-ying, "Inequality Is the Cause of Dissatisfaction" (in Chinese), Ta-hsueh, no. 48, November 1971, p. 42.

78. Cited by Mr. Chang Ching-hang in his statement in "Forum on An Analysis of the Social Forces in Taiwan," the verbatim account of which is in Ta-hsueh, no. 48, November 1971, p. 39.

79. Ibid., p. 28.

80. Ibid., pp. 31-32.

81. Ibid., pp. 35-36.

82. Ibid., p. 30.

83. Chien Chien-chin, "Letter to the Editor," Ta-hsueh, no. 51-52, combined issue, April 1972, p. 7.

84. Wang Wen-yung, "Letter to the Editor" (in Chinese), Ta-hsueh, no. 51-52, p. 6.

85. Huang Sang-lin, "Please Leave the Ivory Tower" (in Chinese), Ta-hsueh, no. 51-52, pp. 65-66.

86. Chu Ping-chin, "The Voice of a Peasant Youth" (in Chinese), Ta-hsueh, no. 54, June 1972, pp. 30-31.

87. Feng Yu-wen, "Also a Voice of a Peasant Youth" (in Chinese), Ta-hsueh, no. 58, October 1972, pp. 53-54.

Chapter II Notes

88. Chen Ku-ying, Wang Shao-po, and Chang Sih-kuo, "Please Save the Children" (in Chinese), <u>Ta-hsueh</u>, no. 59, November 1972.

[illegible faded text]

Chapter III Notes

1. Cited in Hung Shan-hsiang, ed., <u>The Future of the Intellectuals</u> (in Chinese), Taipei, 1973, p. 2. This is a collection of articles from <u>Fa Yen</u> in the years 1971-1973.

2. See Editor(s), "Let Us Make an Experiment" (in Chinese), <u>Ta-hsueh</u>, no. 1, January 1968, p. 1. Also "Our Attitudes and Our Views" (in Chinese), <u>Ta-hsueh</u>, no. 1, pp. 2-3.

3. For Mr. Chang Pao-shu's inspection tour of Taipei, see <u>Chung-yang jih-pao</u>, international edition, November 23, 1970.

4. This writer's interview with Professor Chen Ku-ying.

5. For the list of membership and officials of the journal, see inside cover page, <u>Ta-hsueh</u>, no. 37, January 1971.

6. Yu Hseuh-min, Li Chung-hui, Shih Chih-yang, and Kuan Chung, "Some Opinions on the Previous Issue of the Journal" (in Chinese), <u>Ta-hsueh</u>, no. 38, February 1971, p. 1.

7. Chiang Ching-kuo, "In Memory of My Close Friend Wang Chi-chun" (in Chinese), <u>Ta-hsueh</u>, no. 46, October 1971, pp. 42-50.

8. Wen Tien, "On the Power Struggle in the Nationalist Party: An Analysis of the Third Plenum of the Central Committee" (in Chinese), <u>The United Quarterly</u>, July 1972, New York, p. 17.

Chapter III Notes

9. See inside cover page of <u>Ta-hsueh</u>, no. 49, January 1972.

10. Hungdah Chiu, "The Problems Our Nation Faces After the Withdrawal from the United Nations" (in Chinese), <u>Ta-hsueh</u>, no. 47, November 1971, p. 16.

11. This writer's interview with Professors Yang Kuo-shu and Chen Ku-ying.

12. This is a pen name. The Chinese characters are different, but they sound just the same as the given name of Professor Chen Ku-ying. This type of literary device apparently is still a favorite of Chinese writers.

13. Ku-ying, "The Voice of an Ordinary Citizen" (in Chinese), <u>Chung-yang jih-pao</u>, April 4-April 9, 1972.

14. <u>Ibid.</u>, April 4, 1972.

15. <u>Ibid.</u>, April 6, 1972.

16. <u>Ibid.</u>, April 5, 1972.

17. <u>Ibid.</u>, April 7, 1972.

18. <u>Chung-yang jih-pao</u>, April 15, 1972.

19. Yang Kuo-shu, "The Mentality of False Ease and the Mentality of Rejuvenation" (in Chinese), <u>Ta-hsueh</u>, no. 53, May 1972, p. 56.

20. <u>Hsin-wen tien-ti</u> [News world] 31266, Hong Kong, cited in Chen Ku-ying, preface to <u>Further Thought on Student Movement</u> (in Chinese), Taipei, 1972, p. 3.

21. From this author's notes.

22. Lin Chi-tung, "Letter to the Editor" (in Chinese), <u>Lien Ho-pao</u>, April 28, 1972. Also see Lin Chi-tung, "An Interview with the Editor of <u>Fa Yen</u>" (in Chinese), <u>Ta-hsueh</u>, no. 53, May 1972, p. 32.

Chapter III Notes

23. Wang Wen-hsin, "My View of 'The Voice of an Ordinary Citizen'" (in Chinese), <u>Ta-hsueh</u>, no. 53, May 1972, pp. 33-35.

24. Mab Huang, "On Communication between the Intellectuals and

Taipei, May 1972.

27. Yang Kuo-shu, "The Mentality of False Ease and the Mentality of Rejuvenation" (in Chinese), <u>Ta-hsueh</u>, no. 53, May 1972, p. 55.

28. Yang Kuo-shu, "Trust and Respect Our Youth" (in Chinese), <u>Ta-hsueh</u>, no. 53, pp. 47-52.

29. For example, see Yao Li-min, "Comments on 'The Voice of an Ordinary Citizen'" (in Chinese), <u>The Seventies Monthly</u>, August 1972, Hong Kong, pp. 16-19.

30. From this author's notes on conversation with Professor Chen Ku-ying during his visit with this writer in the early part of August 1972.

31. <u>New York Times</u>, March 16, 1973.

32. <u>Ibid</u>.

33. <u>Ibid</u>.

34. This author's interview with Professor Chen Ku-ying.

35. <u>New York Times</u>, March 16, 1973.

Chapter III Notes

36. "Suspend Our Publication," editorial (in Chinese), Ta-hsueh, no. 63, March-April 1973, p. 1.

37. Ibid.

38. "Letter to the Editor" (in Chinese), Ta-hsueh, no. 64, May 1973, p. 3.

39. Lin Lien-mou, "Letter to the Editor," Ta-hsueh, no. 64, p. 3.

40. Hu Lun-yen, "Letter to the Editor," Ta-hsueh, no. 64, p. 4.

41. "A New Effort," editorial (in Chinese), Ta-hsueh, no. 64, May 1973, pp. 10-11.

42. Chang Ching-hang and Yen Kan-lin, "Various Conceptual Schemes for the Development of Our Country" (in Chinese), Ta-hsueh, no. 65, June 1973, pp. 69-72.

43. For example, see Yen Chao, "What Errors Is the Ta-hsueh tsa-chih Committing?" (in Chinese), Ye-tsao Magazine, combined issue of September-October-November-December 1973, New York, pp. 13-16.

44. Free China Weekly, November 25, 1973.

45. Chang Ching-hang, "An Open Letter to the New Generation" (in Chinese), n.d. This is a campaign pamphlet reprinted in Ye-tsao, no. 22, n.d., New York, p. 32.

46. New York Times, November 25, 1973.

47. Ibid.

48. In "Insight into the Mentality of the Nationalist Party in Its Governing of Taiwan" (in Chinese), a campaign pamphlet, n.d., reprinted in Ye-tsao, no. 22, n.d., New York, pp. 26-28.

49. A campaign pamphlet without title, n.d., reprinted in Ye-tsao, no. 22, n.d., New York, p. 29.

Chapter III Notes

50. New York Times, November 25, 1973.

51. For the account of "The Emergency Meeting of the Philosophy Department of National Taiwan University" (in Chinese), see [illegible]

[illegible]

1. [illegible] Survey, vol. 13, no. 1, January 1973, p. 108.

2. See Chiang Ching-kuo's "Administrative Report to the Legislative Yuan on September 29, 1972," in China Yearbook, 1972-73, pp. 9-10. For a more frank evaluation of the situation by party leaders, see Cha Liang-yung's articles (in Chinese) on his visit to Taiwan in 1973, which appeared in Ming-pao, Hong Kong, June 7-23, 1973. Cha Liang-yung, the publisher of Ming-pao in Hong Kong, visited Taiwan in 1973 and was given an opportunity to interview Vice-President Yen Chia-kan, Chiang Ching-kuo, and other party and government leaders, as well as tour the island.

3. For this point of view, see Hsieh Wen-sun, "A View from Overseas: What Does Chiang Ching-kuo Signify for Taiwan?" (in Chinese), Ta-hsueh, no. 66, July 1973, pp. 5-12. Professor Hsieh Wen-sun teaches at the University of Missouri, St. Louis.

4. For President Chiang Kai-shek's speech at the opening of the National Assembly, see Chung-yang jih-pao, international edition, February 22, 1972. For his speech at the Third Plenum of the Central Committee of the ruling party, see Chung-yang jih-pao, international edition, March 10, 1972.

5. Chung-yang jih-pao, international edition, March 13, 1972.

Chapter IV Notes

6. "After the Amendment to the Temporary Provisions of the Constitution" (in Chinese), editorial, Ta-hsueh, no. 51-52, April 1972, pp. 9-13.

7. For Mr. Ko Cheng-kang's explanation of his intent in using the phrase "the next term," and the adopted resolution, see Chung-yang jih-pao, international edition, March 18, 1972.

8. See China Yearbook, 1972-73, pp. 749-756.

9. Chung-yang jih-pao, international edition, June 29, 1972.

10. See verbatim record of "Forum on National and Local Elections Problems" (in Chinese), Ta-hsueh, no. 56, August 1972, pp. 31-70. This forum was sponsored by the Ta-hsueh tsachih on July 7, 1972. About fifty persons participated, including this writer.

11. "On Substantial Reduction of the Number of Additional Members of the People's Representatives" (in Chinese), editorial, Ta-hsueh, no. 54, June 1972, pp. 9-10.

12. "Forum on National and Local Elections Problems," pp. 32-33, 36.

13. Ibid., p. 33.

14. Ibid., p. 40.

15. See Chung-yang jih-pao, international edition, September 22, September 23, December 7, December 8, 1972.

16. Chung-yang jih-pao, international edition, September 23, 1972.

17. New York Times, November 5, 1972.

18. Ibid.

19. New York Times, November 12, 1972.

Chapter IV Notes

20. Ibid.

21. For the results of the elections, see Chung-yang jih-pao, international edition, December 25, 1972. Also China Year-

[lines illegible]

25. See the verbatim account of "The Forum on a Reevaluation of the Elections" (in Chinese), Ta-hsueh, no. 62, February 1973, pp. 11-33.

26. Ibid., p. 14, p. 16, p. 17.

27. Chia Pao (J. Bruce Jacobs), "The View of an American on the Elections in Taiwan" (in Chinese), Ta-hsueh, no. 62, February 1973, p. 37.

28. Ibid., p. 38.

29. "The Forum on a Reevaluation of Elections," p. 26.

30. "Take a Long View of Elections" (in Chinese), editorial, Ta-hsueh, no. 62, February 1973, p. 6.

31. Ibid., p. 9.

32. Chung-yang jih-pao, international edition, May 18, 1972.

33. Ibid.

34. For the composition of the new cabinet and the appointment of governor of Taiwan and mayor of Taipei, see Chung-yang jih-pao, international edition, May 30, 1972.

Chapter IV Notes

35. Ibid.

36. "On the Inspiring Chiang Ching-kuo's Cabinet" (in Chinese), editorial, Ta-hsueh, no. 54, June 1972, pp. 6-7. Also see Han Wei, "New Man and New Spirit in the Executive Yuan" (in Chinese), Chung-yang jih-pao, international edition, May 30, 1972.

37. See Chung-yang jih-pao, international edition, May 16, 1972.

38. Ibid.

39. Chung-yang jih-pao, international edition, June 19, 1973.

40. Chung-yang jih-pao, international edition, May 31, 1973.

41. Chung-yang jih-pao, international edition, June 28, 1973.

42. See "The Prospect of National Progress," editorial, Ta-hsueh, no. 65, June 1973, p. 9.

43. Chung-yang jih-pao, international edition, June 9, November 22, December 12, 1972.

44. Chung-yang jih-pao, international edition, September 28, November 16, November 26, 1972.

45. Chung-yang jih-pao, international edition, November 14, 1972; June 18, 1973.

46. For example, see his nine-point instructions to Mayor of Taipei Chang Feng-shu as to reform measures, Chung-yang jih-pao, international edition, July 18, 1972.

47. See Chung-yang jih-pao, November 22, December 12, 1972.

48. Chung-yang jih-pao, international edition, June 9, 1972.

49. Chung-yang jih-pao, international edition, June 25, 1972.

50. Chung-yang jih-pao, international edition, June 10, 1972.

Chapter IV Notes

51. Ibid.

52. Chung-yang jih-pao, international edition, June 25, 1972.

58. Chung-kuo shih-pao, July 18, 1973.

59. Chung-yang jih-pao, international edition, March 7, 1973.

60. China Yearbook, 1972-73, p. 321.

61. For an analysis of this conference, see Chen Yung-teh, "An Analysis of Youth Attitude at the Present Time: A Survey of the Reactions of Participants in the Summer Conference of National Construction" (in Chinese), Ta-hsueh, no. 46, October 1971, pp. 35-41.

62. Ibid., p. 35.

63. Ibid., p. 36.

64. From this author's notes.

65. Chung-yang jih-pao, international edition, March 30, 1972.

66. Chung-yang jih-pao, international edition, September 28, 1972.

67. Chung-yang jih-pao, international edition, November 16, 1972.

68. Chung-yang jih-pao, international edition, May 30, 1973.

69. Ibid.

Chapter IV Notes

70. Chung-yang jih-pao, international edition, August 26, 1973.

71. Chung-yang jih-pao, international edition, January 6, 1973.

72. Chung-yang jih-pao, international edition, February 9, 1973.

73. Chung-yang jih-pao, international edition, July 11, 1973; March 11, 1974.

74. Chung-yang jih-pao, international edition, September 28, 1973.

75. Ibid.

76. Chung-yang jih-pao, international edition, November 5, 1972.

77. Chung-yang jih-pao, international edition, March 21, 1973.

78. Chung-yang jih-pao, international edition, April 21, 1973.

79. Chung-yang jih-pao, international edition, March 13, 1973; August 23, 1973.

80. See editorial, Chung-yang jih-pao, international edition, September 28, 1972; also editorial, Lien-ho jih-pao, March 22, 1973.

81. "The Meaning of Accelerating Rural Construction at This Stage" (in Chinese), editorial, Ta-hsueh, no. 58, October 1972, pp. 5-6.

82. Chung-yang jih-pao, March 25, 1973.

83. Chung-yang jih-pao, international edition, April 26, 1973.

84. Chung-yang jih-pao, international edition, June 2, 1973.

85. Ibid.

86. Chung-yang jih-pao, international edition, June 15, 1973.

87. Ibid.

Chapter IV Notes

88. <u>Chung-yang jih-pao</u>, international edition, June 23, 1973.

89. <u>Chung-yang jih-pao</u>, international edition, March 9, 1974.

MICHIGAN PAPERS IN CHINESE STUDIES

No. 1. The Chinese Economy, 1912-1949, by Albert Feuerwerker.

No. 2. The Cultural Revolution: 1967 in Review, four essays by

No. 6. Chinese Paintings in Chinese Publications, 1956-1968: An Annotated Bibliography and an Index to the Paintings, by E. J. Laing.

No. 7. The Treaty Ports and China's Modernization: What Went Wrong? by Rhoads Murphey.

No. 8. Two Twelfth Century Texts on Chinese Painting, by Robert J. Maeda.

No. 9. The Economy of Communist China, 1949-1969, by Chu-yuan Cheng.

No. 10. Educated Youth and the Cultural Revolution in China, by Martin Singer.

No. 11. Premodern China: A Bibliographical Introduction, by Chun-shu Chang.

No. 12. Two Studies on Ming History, by Charles O. Hucker.

No. 13. Nineteenth Century China: Five Imperialist Perspectives, selected by Dilip Basu, edited by Rhoads Murphey.

No. 14. Modern China, 1840-1972: An Introduction to Sources and Research Aids, by Andrew J. Nathan.

No. 15. Women in China: Studies in Social Change and Feminism, edited by Marilyn B. Young.

No. 16. An Annotated Bibliography of Chinese Painting Catalogues and Related Texts, by Hin-cheung Lovell.

No. 17. China's Allocation of Fixed Capital Investment, 1952-1957, by Chu-yuan Cheng.

No. 18. Health, Conflict, and the Chinese Political System, by David M. Lampton.

No. 19. Chinese and Japanese Music-Dramas, edited by J. I. Crump and William P. Malm.

No. 20. Hsin-lun (New Treatise) and Other Writings by Huan T'an (43 B.C.-28 A.D.), translated by Timoteus Pokora.

No. 21. Rebellion in Nineteenth-Century China, by Albert Feuerwerker.

No. 22. Between Two Plenums: China's Intraleadership Conflict, 1959-1962, by Ellis Joffe.

No. 23. "Proletarian Hegemony" in the Chinese Revolution and the Canton Commune of 1927, by S. Bernard Thomas.

No. 24. Chinese Communist Materials at the Bureau of Investigation Archives, Taiwan, by Peter Donovan, Carl E. Dorris, and Lawrence R. Sullivan.

No. 25. Shanghai Old-Style Banks (Ch'ien-chuang), 1800-1935, by Andrea Lee McElderry.

No. 26. The Sian Incident: A Pivotal Point in Modern Chinese History, by Tien-wei Wu.

No. 27. State and Society in Eighteenth-Century China: The Ch'ing Empire in Its Glory, by Albert Feuerwerker.

No. 28. Intellectual Ferment for Political Reforms in Taiwan, 1971-1973, by Mab Huang.

No. 29. The Foreign Establishment in China in the Early Twentieth Century, by Albert Feuerwerker.

MICHIGAN ABSTRACTS OF CHINESE AND JAPANESE WORKS ON CHINESE HISTORY

No. 1. The Ming Tribute Grain System, by Hoshi Ayao, translated by Mark Elvin.

No. 5. The Silk Industry in Ch'ing China, by Shih Min-hsiung, translated by E-tu Zen Sun.

NONSERIES PUBLICATION

Index to the "Chan-kuo Ts'e," by Sharon Fidler and J. I. Crump. A companion volume to the Chan-kuo Ts'e, translated by J. I. Crump (Oxford: Clarendon Press, 1970).

Michigan Papers and Abstracts available from:
Center for Chinese Studies
The University of Michigan
Lane Hall (Publications)
Ann Arbor, MI 48109 USA

Prepaid Orders Only
write for complete price listing